Safe Haven

Ethnocultural Voices Series

Multicultural History Society of Ontario

Published with the assistance of the Ontario Ministry of Citizenship and the Ministry of Culture, Tourism and Recreation.

The views expressed in this publication represent the experiences and opinions of the individual contributors and not necessarily those of the Ministry of Citizenship, the Ministry of Culture, Tourism and Recreation, or the Multicultural History Society of Ontario.

Safe Haven

The Refugee Experience of Five Families

Edited by Elizabeth McLuhan

Multicultural History Society of Ontario

Canadian Cataloguing in Publication Data

Safe haven : the refugee experience of five families

(Ethnocultural voices)
ISBN 0-919045-67-7

1. Refugees, Political – Canada – Biography.
2. Minorities – Canada – Biography. 3. Refugees –
Government policy – Canada. 4. Canada – Emigration
and immigration – Government policy. I. McLuhan,
Elizabeth. II. Multicultural History Society of Ontario. III. Series.

JV7282.R43S3 1995   325.21'092'271   C95–931081–9

Cover design by Kathy Cloutier, University of Toronto Press
Design and layout by Catherine A. Waite, Polished Prose
Printed and bound by the University of Toronto Press

Safe Haven **is available from:**
University of Toronto Press
5201 Dufferin Street
North York, Ontario
Canada M3H 5T8
Order Fulfillment 1-800-565-9523

Contents

Preface   vii
    Milton Israel

In Search of Safe Haven   1
    Harold Troper

Czechs/Slovaks   19
    The Straznicky Family
      Eva Marha
    The Straznicky Family Speaks
      Eva Marha
    The Czech/Slovak Community
      Eva Marha

Chileans   65
    The Enriquez Family
      Carlos Piña and Elizabeth McLuhan
    The Enriquez Family Speaks
      Carlos Piña and Elizabeth McLuhan
    The Chilean Community
      Andrew Israel

Vietnamese   115
    The Pham Family
      Jennifer Khong
    The Pham Family Speaks
      Jennifer Khong
    The Vietnamese Community
      Jennifer Khong

044523

Sri Lankan Tamils   145
    The Segaran Family
        Sujata Ramachandran
    The Segaran Family Speaks
        Sujata Ramachandran
    The Sri Lankan Tamil Community
        Arul Aruliah

Somalis   181
    The Abdi Family
        Edward Opaku-Dapaah and Elizabeth McLuhan
    The Abdi Family Speaks
        Edward Opaku-Dapaah and Elizabeth McLuhan
    The Somali Community
        Edward Opaku-Dapaah

Further Readings   219

Acknowledgments   220

The Safe Haven Exhibition   223
    Paul Robert Magocsi

Afterword   226
    Elizabeth McLuhan

Photo Credits   229

Preface

This book is many things. It is a description of a project of research and outreach, and the establishment of a creative new relationship between the Multicultural History Society of Ontario and the Royal Ontario Museum. Safe Haven was the inaugural show (November 1993 through August 1995) of the Heritage Gallery of Canada's Peoples, a new ROM Gallery that is managed in partnership by the MHSO and ROM. It is also the script of a series of interviews of five refugee families who found a safe haven in Canada and share the story of the troubles that drove them from their countries, the trauma of the journey, and the challenges of resettlement. It is as well a story about all of us as Canadians, of our being and becoming, of our nation still in the making, and of how it is trying to define and protect a secure sense of itself at the same time.

Canada's commitment to remain open to a continuing flow of immigrants and refugees is a reflection of the mix of self-interest and generosity of spirit with which we identify ourselves at home and in the world. We want and need immigrants to continue the building of our society and economy. And we are determined to inform our response to those who need a safe haven with a commitment to share our wealth and freedom. The difficulties are clear, as are the limits of our capacity to respond to the increasing numbers who are no longer at home anywhere in the world. We remain, however, among the most open, the most generous and, as a result both now and potentially, among the most benefited of peoples. This book is a small contribution to the story and to the debate. Elizabeth McLuhan's vision and administrative skills were essential to the success of the project. She developed the ideas and was fully engaged in the demanding task of implementing them in the exhibition that she curated, and in this book that she edited. The Multicultural History Society of Ontario is pleased to provide this opportunity to hear these voices and to recognize them as our own.

Milton Israel
Chairman, Board of Directors
Multicultural History Society of Ontario

In Search of Safe Haven

In recent years, Canada has led Western nations in offering safe haven to those who require it. The passion with which nation-states around the world inflict suffering on their own citizens has created millions of refugees. Conservative estimates count 30 million people who are currently in flight for fear of persecution in their homelands. The majority are women and children. One can only guess at how many more would take refuge elsewhere if there were an "elsewhere" to which they could escape, or if the persecution they endure did not foreclose the possibility of escape. And although it is essential to keep statistics on the global refugee crisis so that international aid personnel can track the flow of refugees and allocate necessary resources, these horrific numbers may also make it difficult for even the most caring Canadian to relate to the refugee issue.

When faced with the spectre of tens of millions at risk, can one be faulted for concluding that the world refugee crisis is so large that only governments acting in concert can deal with it? What impact can any one Canadian have in the face of such human tragedy? And with tens of millions in need of a safe haven, can opening Canada's doors to one refugee or even five families make a difference?

There can be no other answer. Yes. When confronted by such statistics, it is imperative that one not lose sight of the fact that each of those tens of millions is a single person. Indeed, it is said that by saving one life, it is as if you have saved the world.

No doubt R 5001 3210 would understand. Who is R 5001 3210? He is (or rather he was) a refugee. In 1980 he fled from the certainty of political repression in Vietnam into the unknown future of a Thai refugee camp. To friends and family left behind in Vietnam, he was Pham, Thê Trung, a creative man who spoke eloquently through the artistic imagination that remains his voice. The perilous sea voyage in a 10-metre-long fishing boat that brought him and fifty-eight other exhausted escapees to asylum in Thailand cost him more than his life's savings. It threatened to rob him of his sense of place, his roots, and his identity. In the Thai refugee camp where he was placed, Pham, Thê Trung became R 5001 3210, just one more refugee case file among all the others waiting to be processed.

What would become of him? He had made one of the most difficult decisions he would ever have to make–to flee his home. He had taken his life and a few possessions in his own hands and now, as a refugee, the power to determine his future was in the hands of others. Memories of Vietnam faded as R 5001 3210 hoped for a new tomorrow. He applied to come to Canada and waited for his number to come up on a list of those to be permanently resettled in a land where he might again be known as Pham, Thê Trung.

But what made Pham, Thê Trung a refugee? Indeed, what is a refugee? For many of us the term "refugee" is commonly applied to individuals and groups who are forced by disaster or deprivation, whether at the hand of nature or their fellow citizens, to flee. They leave behind their homes, often their families, and the comfort of all that is familiar.

But definitions are more than just ways of describing phenomena. They have legal implications, and this widely accepted definition of a refugee is not sufficiently narrow to pinpoint those the international community was prepared to recognize and process. The 1951 United Nations Convention relating to the Status of Refugees, to which Canada became a signatory in 1969, sets out two conditions for validating an individual's claim to be a refugee and, therefore, entitling him or her to the protection afforded refugees by the United Nations Convention. One condition relates to the refugee claimant's reasons for flight, while the other relates to the individual's location. Convention refugees are defined as "persons who are outside their country because of a well-founded fear of persecution for reasons of race, religion, nationality, membership of a political social group or political opinion." There is no room in this definition for victims of economic decay, environmental degradation, or even natural disaster.

Some countries, like Canada, which subscribe to the two-part United Nations Convention definition–that one has a well-founded fear of persecution and is outside his or her country of citizenship–have incorporated the definition into immigration legislation. But some countries, again including Canada, also allow for a humanitarian expansion of the definition (where conditions might warrant) to include so-called designated classes of individuals–for example, those who have a well-founded fear, if not a demonstrated experience of persecution, but who have not been able to escape their country of citizenship, might otherwise be permitted into Canada for humanitarian reasons.

And what are the responsibilities of countries that have signed the United Nations Convention? Several major points stand out. These countries pledge to offer sanctuary to those who are judged to fall under the Convention definition. It also means that these countries accept the principle of *non-refoulement*, that is, they must not return an individual to a country where he or she will suffer persecution. Buttressing the definition and the obligations of different countries are all the procedures for determining who is a genuine refugee and, therefore, who is entitled to the protection of the United Nations Convention and what to do about those who are not. In the past, most refugees have been repatriated to their country of origin once conditions permitted their safe return. But what is to be done with those who will probably never be able to go home or who do not wish to go and, as a result, may end their days in crowded refugee camps, unable to settle in the society that gives them temporary asylum? It is in such situations that nations like Canada have played an especially important role as countries of second asylum, offering refugees new homes, new hope, and new citizenship.

In recent years, Canada has not been just a country of second asylum. It has also become a country of first asylum as individuals seeking a safe harbour from persecution make their way to Canada and request asylum. In such cases, Canada has been forced to develop its own procedures for determining who is and who is not a refugee. But whether as a country of first or second asylum, Canada and Canadians are now major players in determining the plight of refugees throughout the world. Since the end of World War II, almost half a million refugees have come to Canada to reclaim their lives.

In 1980, R 5001 3210 was approved for resettlement in Canada. He reclaimed his life and his name–Pham, Thê Trung. The story of Pham, Thê Trung is celebrated in this book together with those of other individual refugees or refugee families who found safe haven in Canada from the strife of the former Czechoslovakia, Chile, Somalia, and Sri Lanka. What do they and thousands of other refugees who sought refuge in Canada have in common? Many came to Canada under special resettlement programs or provisions of the immigration law designed to alleviate the plight of refugees by offering Canada as a new home and, in the process, they bound their futures together with all other Canadians.

It was not always thus. During the worst refugee crisis of the modern era–the years of Nazi terror–Canada was found wanting. For those who would ultimately be consigned to the death camps and crematoria, an uncaring world was divided into two parts: a part where they dared not stay and a part that they could not enter. Canada was among the latter. It offered no haven and was determined to ignore the pleas of those for whom rejection meant certain death.

In the years since World War II, Canada has gradually emerged as one of the world's major refugee-receiving nations, but this transition has not been smooth or universally embraced by past Canadian governments or the Canadian people. Indeed, for much of the past fifty years, Canada had no active refugee policy. On the contrary, Canada resisted the notion that it should be a haven to the persecuted. Canada admitted refugees, but until the late 1970s, Canada made no specific provision in law to do so. Those persons in flight from fear of persecution who were admitted into Canada, including refugees from the Hungarian uprising of 1956 and the Soviet repression of the Prague Spring in 1967, were admitted, in part, because they were able to satisfy exacting conditions placed on regular immigrants or because a specific exception to the immigration legislation was approved by Cabinet. Only in the late 1970s did Canada change its immigration policy and law to offer asylum to those with a legitimate fear of persecution and, as a result, affirm an ongoing commitment to resettlement in Canada as a legal and moral responsibility.

How did this change in policy, law, and attitude come about? Certainly there was little to encourage change in this direction in the immediate post-World War II era. While the cheers of victory celebrations still echoed in their ears, most Canadians gave little thought to postwar refugees or any other would-be immigrants. A wall of restriction kept most people out. Existing laws prohibited immigration of Asians and restricted immigration from eastern and southern Europe; nor was there any public clamour to open Canada's door to refugees, especially not to the hundreds of thousands of Displaced Persons (DPs) who were temporarily sheltered in camps in Germany, Austria, and Italy. Instead, Canada initially approved of the repatriation of DPs back to their original countries of citizenship. The government reasoned that if everyone went home, there would be no DPs. When it became obvious that as many as a million persons would not voluntarily return home, in particular Jewish holocaust survivors for whom Europe was a massive graveyard and eastern Europeans who rejected return to homelands that were by then under Soviet domination, Canadian authorities denied that Canada had any obligation, moral or otherwise, to offer new homes to the homeless.

But thousands of DPs did eventually enter Canada as part of a major economic expansion of Canada's labour force. Indeed, throughout most of the postwar decades, the single most important factor influencing Canadian policy was economic self-interest. At the end of the war, without the stimulant of massive war-related spending, many policy planners anticipated that Canada and the West in general would slip back into a 1930s-like depression. But they were wrong. After a lurching start, the postwar Canadian economy expanded rapidly. For the first time since the onset of the Great Depression, the problem was a shortage of goods, not money; of labour, not jobs.

Of course, not all Canadians agreed that building prosperity with the labour of immigrants who were previously considered undesirable on racial and ethnic grounds, especially Jewish and Slavic DPs, was a good idea. Barely a year after the end of World War II, a public opinion poll found that Canadians preferred Germans over Jews as immigrants. Only the Japanese, the other of Canada's major wartime enemies, fared worse than Jews.

But the industrial sectors needed labour and immigration was a prime source of it. When it became apparent that the United Kingdom, the United States, and western Europe (particularly the Netherlands) could not fill all of Canada's labour needs, the government and labour-intensive industries were forced to look further afield. Business warned that the economic boom hinged on imported labour and pressed Ottawa to skim off the cream of the labour pool languishing in the DP camps of Europe. While they began processing candidates in DP camps, immigration officials remained mindful of the Canadian public's desire to ensure that arrivals, including refugees, be "racially" acceptable. As they scoured the DP camps of Europe for immigrants, prospects were judged in a descending order of ethnic preference. Refugees from the Baltic republics (Estonia, Latvia, Lithuania), described as hard-working "Nordic types," were ranked higher than Slavic applicants, and Slavs ranked higher than Jews. In holding fast to their ethnic hierarchy of admissibility, immigration personnel were following Prime Minister Mackenzie King's lead. In May 1947, as Canada first began processing immigration applications, including those of refugees from the Displaced Persons camps of Europe, the prime minister reflected well the national mood when he cautioned that "the people of Canada do not wish to make a fundamental alteration in the character of their people through mass immigration."

Gradually, however, with the market for labour in Canada still strong and government officials satisfied that the Canadian public was more receptive to the arrival of DPs than originally anticipated, larger numbers of Jews and other eastern Europeans previously regarded as undesirable were admitted. But there were limits to Canada's new openness and these limits were also racial. Restrictions against Asians and other non-whites remained intact.

For ten years after the end of World War II, thousands of those displaced by the political turmoil of postwar Europe came to Canada. They found homes and rebuilt their lives. In the process, they provided much of the labour needed to drive the Canadian economy and helped chart Canada's social and cultural life for a generation to come. Their contribution to Canada is beyond calculation, as has been that of the refugee stream that followed.

In 1956, as the DP camps of Europe were finally closed, other refugee camps suddenly opened. When Soviet tanks rolled into Budapest to crush the Hungarian uprising, they also set off a flood of refugees who escaped westward into Austria. This first refugee crisis of a deepening Cold War era came at a fortuitous moment for Canada. Its economy was still buoyant and the demand for immigrant labour strong, but official Ottawa remained cautious. Canadian security personnel warned that the Soviets might use any refugee resettlement program to slip subversives into Western democracies like Canada. The Canadian government, however, seemed less concerned about spies than about costs. Who would pay for any Hungarian resettlement program?

While the government pondered its options, national media

attention remained focused on the plight of Hungarian "freedom fighters." Their defeat and scramble to find sanctuary in Austria touched the heart of Cold War Canada. The public's demand that the government do its part in resettling these Hungarian refugees increased. Private organizations pledged money to cover the costs, and the press assaulted the government for its dithering in the face of human misery. Bowing to pressure, the government finally announced it would set aside or postpone routine immigration procedures, including some medical and security checks, so as to speed Hungarian entry into Canada. The minister of immigration flew to Vienna, followed by teams of immigration officials who were intent on skimming off the cream of Hungarian refugees for Canada before other countries got them. Before the movement ended, 37,000 Hungarians joined the Canadian community; Canada admitted proportionately more Hungarian refugees than any other country.

At the time, officials believed this emergency refugee resettlement program would be a one-time exception to the regular routine of Canadian immigration. Unfortunately, persecution and state terror did not end with the Hungarian episode. In 1968, a flickering light of liberal reform in the former Czechoslovakia, known as the Prague Spring, was extinguished under the heel of yet another Soviet military action, but this was not a repeat of the Hungarian revolt. Fearing the kind of blood bath that Hungarians had endured, the Czechoslovak government and its peoples offered little armed resistance to the Soviets, who moved quickly to reassert control. But as Soviet armour closed Czechoslovakia off from the West, thousands raced for border points, hoping to cross the frontier before Soviet authorities sealed off avenues of escape. Others, stunned by the suddenness of the Soviet action, were too late. They were locked inside a Czechoslovakia where state repression was now the order of the day.

Some, like the Straznicky family, who did not leave before the frontiers were sealed off, were determined not to live out their lives in a Soviet-dominated Czechoslovakia. The Straznickys carefully and secretly began plotting their escape. It was a dangerous process. They knew that any slip, any suspicion that they aroused, could turn their dream of freedom into the nightmare of arrest and prison. But the Straznicky family was luckier than most. With more resources and a wider circle of connections than many others, their plan worked. All of them—Ivan, Marta (who was pregnant), and their five children—got out. They left behind all their possessions, their extended family, and their friends, but they still considered themselves fortunate. Others failed and paid a heavy price.

The Straznickys joined approximately 12,000 other Czechoslovakian refugees admitted to Canada. Unlike the Hungarian episode a decade earlier, the Canadian government was quick to respond to the crisis of refugees from Czechoslovakia. Driven by a mixture of Cold War crusading, altruistic concern for the suffering of others, and the self-serving prospect of reaping yet another rich harvest of educated and talented people, Ottawa hurried to get its share of the Czech and Slovak refugees before they were scooped up by others.

Despite their differences, the Hungarian and Czech/Slovak refugee episodes underscored several overlapping points. The first of these is that Canada had no systematically planned or organized response to refugees around the world. In spite of Canada's high-profile role at the United Nations, a legacy of the Lester Pearson years, and even after signing the United Nations Convention relating to the Status of Refugees in 1969, it was not until almost a decade later that Canada made a commitment in law to offer asylum to those in distress. In the meantime, Canada's response was ad hoc. Indeed, the Hungarian and Czechoslovak refugee resettlement episodes were regarded at the time as exceptions to Canadian immigration practice. And, to be honest, if the government and immigration officials had any singular vision of refugees, it was less as an immediate issue of humanitarian concern to be addressed with compassion than as a long-term economic opportunity to be tapped for Canada's benefit. Refugees, like other immigrants, were an investment. For Canada, it seemed as important to do well as to do good.

In fact, in both the Hungarian and Czechoslovak cases, Canada did do well, but there were limits on Canada's readiness to welcome even skilled and educated refugees. Like the refugee problem itself, one important limit was tied to politics. It is hard to avoid the conclusion that while the suffering endured by the persecuted may be similar, the political source of their pain made a difference in the eyes of Canadian authorities. It was widely acknowledged that when it came to resettling refugees in Canada, the government favoured those from communist or other high-profile and unpopular regimes over those from equally repressive right-wing persecution. For example, there was an obvious discrepancy between Canada's response to Idi Amin's 1972 ruthless mass expulsion of Ugandan Asians who had lived in Uganda for generations and the systematic Chilean repression of all political dissent after the 1973 right-wing *coup d'etat* against Salvador Allende's democratically elected left-wing government.

In the case of the approximately 50,000 Asians with British passports who were expelled from Uganda by Idi Amin, the British, hoping to avoid a backlash against the arrival in Britain of thousands of Asians, appealed to Canada and other countries for assistance. To its credit, Canada, which had several years earlier officially expunged racial and ethnic discrimination from its immigration law and procedures, responded in the affirmative. Immigration authorities swung into action. By the time the Ugandan resettlement program ended, Canada had admitted more than 7,000 Ugandan Asians. The group was predominantly made up of younger, well-educated professionals and entrepreneurs who, it was judged, would do well in Canada.

The Ugandan resettlement program contrasts with the Chilean experience a year later. Canadian immigration policy may have become colour-blind to race, but not to ideology. And when it came to Chileans, immigration and security personnel saw red. After the overthrow of Allende's democratically elected socialist government in an American-supported coup in September 1973, Canada, protecting major Canadian investment in Chile, was among the first to recognize Augusto Pinochet's military regime. Canadian investment may have been safe, but those who had supported the recently ousted Allende government or who might otherwise be considered unfriendly to the new regime were far less so. Arrests, "disappearances," and political repression marked a reign of terror as the new regime demonstrated its unwillingness to tolerate any political opposition or to forgive those who had supported the ousted Allende government.

But if Canadian officials hoped all this would be kept at arm's length—an unpleasant and distant Chilean problem best left to the Chileans to work out—they were wrong. It soon became a Canadian problem when a small band of desperate Chileans entered the Canadian embassy in Santiago to beg for political asylum refused to leave.

Among them was a prominent professor of English literature at the University of Chile, who was a university official and Allende supporter. Immediately following the coup, the police began to hunt for Belisario Enriquez. He went into hiding. He had little illusion about what would happen to him if he were caught. Friends had been found murdered. Others were arrested, tortured, or never heard from again. The National Stadium in Santiago was converted into a huge prison. To avoid being picked up, Enriquez moved from safe house to safe house, while his wife and three children lay low at home. Finally, with the help of an official from the French embassy, which was already crowded with asylum seekers and surrounded by Chilean security personnel, Enriquez slipped into the Canadian embassy. Together with others whose lives were in danger, he refused to leave.

As embassy officials struggled to cope with their unwanted guests, Ottawa seemed unsure of how to proceed. Certainly Canada did not want to set a precedent by rewarding those who invaded its embassies, no matter what the threat, with admission to Canada. Canada also did not want to be perceived as unfriendly to the new   Chilean military regime or its major supporter, the United States. But Canada also did not want to be seen turning away those who were truly in danger.

If the Canadian government was unsure of how to proceed, there were Canadians who knew exactly what they wanted their government to do, and they were determined that their government should respond with a generosity of heart. A vocal lobby, led by church groups, began pressuring Ottawa to accept significant numbers of Chileans who were facing torture or imprisonment for their political views. Whether to placate these lobbyists or just to clear the embassy, arrangements were made with the Chilean government to allow a single Canadian Forces plane to fly into Santiago in January 1974 and bring out the embassy refugees and their families, including Belisario Enriquez, his wife Maria Angelica Nuñez, and their three children. One hundred twenty-eight people were brought to safe haven in Canada.

But this flight did not begin a major movement to Canada. In comparison with the Ugandan Asian refugee resettlement program or the earlier Czechoslovak and Hungarian programs, commitment to action seemed lacking. In spite of continuing pressure from support groups in Canada, immigration officials were reluctant to set up shop in Santiago or to cut corners in processing the departure of those who were under constant threat of arrest and torture. And while one cannot minimize the difficulty of organizing the removal of persons from *within* their country of origin, one can also not escape the conclusion that Canadian authorities were uneasy about accepting any large group of potentially left-leaning immigrants or concerned about a negative American or Chilean government reaction. Once approval for a removal program was granted, immigration authorities were accused of burying applications under a mountain of paperwork. For some Chileans, just applying to leave Chile for Canada was dangerous. Still, Canadian officials were not prepared to waive security checks as they had done in the earlier Hungarian and Czechoslovak episodes.

Two years after the overthrow of Allende and in spite of a

continuing international censure of the Chilean dictatorship's wholesale abuse of political and human rights, fewer than 2,000 Chileans were cleared for entry into Canada. Gradually, removals increased. In the end, almost 7,000 Chileans finally made it into Canada. Many of them were the kind of educated, white-collar professionals who, in different times, might have successfully applied to Canada as immigrants. This is not to argue that Chilean refugees were any more or less deserving of Canadian asylum than Ugandan Asians. On the contrary, the Chilean case clearly illustrates that just as Canada's response to humanitarian abuse could be tempered by economic self-interest, economic self-interest could also be tempered by political considerations.

As the numbers of individuals and groups suffering persecution increased, and as one refugee crisis overlapped another, Canadian officials came to see the need for a national refugee policy that would be in line with those of its Western allies, one that would allow Canada to prepare and respond to refugees around the world in an ongoing and orderly way. Certainly, Canada could no longer respond to crises in the ad hoc fashion that characterized previous decades. Parliament responded. In a new Immigration Act that came into effect in 1978, Canada, for the first time, recognized refugees as a distinct class of immigrants, separate from other immigrants and entitled to Canadian asylum. In administrative terms, this meant that a percentage of an annual immigration target was to be set aside each year for refugees. But, in effect, two routes opened up to refugees: an off shore route in which Canadian authorities continue to go abroad, often to refugee camps, to select from among those who were already granted Convention refugee status; and secondly, an internal route by which individuals, who make their way to Canada on their own, claim refugee status once they arrive in Canada. The internal route demanded that Canada organize and maintain a system for determining the legitimacy of individual claims.

The new Immigration Act's off shore refugee provisions were almost immediately put to the test during the Vietnamese boat people crisis of 1978. It was hard to steel one's heart against the media's horrific images of weary men, women, and children packed onto tiny wooden vessels in a desperate search for a safe harbour. It is still unclear why so many Canadians were so touched by the particular agony of the boat people–including Pham, Thê Trung-but a public clamour for Canadian action grew. Thousands of individuals across Canada linked with friends, neighbours, and church groups to forge a chain of support for Vietnamese refugees. If they were not a majority of Canadians, they represented a grass roots organization the likes of which Canada had never seen. Tapping into refugee sponsorship provisions of the new Immigration Act, small groups came together and applied to bring refugee families to Canada. At first taken aback by the magnitude of public distress at events in Southeast Asia, Ottawa soon responded with humanity and dispatch. By the end of 1980, the government united with private refugee sponsorship groups across Canada to admit more than 60,000 Vietnamese, Cambodian, Laotians, and ethnic Chinese from Southeast Asia. This is reportedly the highest per capita resettlement program of any country.

Since the boat people episode, refugee admissions have remained an important and often controversial part of Canada's overall immigration program. Throughout the 1980s, Canada continued to be a mainstay in refugee resettlement among Western receiving countries, so much so that Canadians remain the only people who have been collectively awarded the Nansen Medal from the United Nations for its "sustained contribution ... to the cause of refugees." In 1980, at the height of the boat people crisis, the annual estimate of refugees had to be increased to slightly more than 28 per cent of all immigrants admitted to Canada. During the subsequent ten years, the percentage of refugees hovered between 14 and 20 per cent of all admissions to Canada.

Among those refugees who found new homes in Canada during the 1980s were many who were escaping from the political decay of eastern Europe, Yugoslavia, Southeast Asia, and the seemingly never-ending civil strife of Central America. Joining them were Tamil refugees escaping the bloody civil strife of Sri Lanka. In response to anti-Tamil riots in the streets of Colombo, the Sri Lankan capital, the Canadian government introduced in 1983 a special Tamil refugee resettlement program. Some were selected from among those who escaped government-sanctioned terror by making their way to the temporary safety of refugee camps in Jaffna, to the northern Tamil-dominated areas of Sri Lanka, or by sea across the Palk Strait to southern India. Others took different escape routes. Denied the protection of their government, some travelled on expensive false documents.

For the Segaran family, the riots in Colombo changed their world forever. With her husband Siva working abroad, Indira Segaran and her three children barely escaped Colombo alive. Their possessions were looted and their home was burned. They made their way northward to Jaffna and eventually to India. With the return of peace, the Segarans returned to Colombo, but soon realized that as Tamils they would not be able to rebuild a life secure from threat in Sri Lanka. Siva left Sri Lanka and found his way to Canada by a roundabout route through Europe on false papers. He claimed refugee status. His application was granted and he soon brought his family to join him in Canada.

Siva was not alone. In 1983, the first year of Canada's Tamil resettlement program, more than 1,800 Tamils were admitted. In the years that followed, thousands more who had lost their homes, most of them women and many of them victims of rape or torture, have tried to build new lives for their families in Canada.

But would this path be open to others to travel? As the 1980s drew to a close and an economic malaise took hold, the public mood showed signs of unease on the issue of refugees. Could it be that, following the nation's unprecedented burst of humanitarian zeal during the boat people crisis, enthusiasm was spent? Perhaps uneasy at the onset of an economic slow-down, Canadians seemed too drained to concern themselves with the trials of others. Perhaps Canadians were responding uneasily to the dramatic shift that was the by-product of refugee immigration since the early 1970s and that was increasingly visible in the streets of major Canadian cities: the majority of new arrivals were not white. Whatever the reason or combination of reasons, anxiety gradually focused on those refugee claimants who were not selected abroad by immigration officials but who claimed refugee status once they arrived in Canada. Too often, they were incorrectly seen as "abusing the system," somehow violating Canadian sovereignty and the rules that determined who should enter Canada. Canada did not choose them. They chose Canada. As the line of refugee claimants within Canada grew longer, the refugee determination review system, which was never designed to handle a large volume of applicants, was hard pressed to keep pace. Fears of system overload were compounded by exaggerated reports of fraudulent refugee claimants with no "well-founded fear of persecution" who used Canada's refugee program to "sneak into Canada through the back door." It was not long before public muttering about tightening up the refugee determination review system could be heard. While human rights and pro-refugee activists lobbied to ensure that those in danger would not be denied asylum, government officials, intent on making the refugee review procedure more efficient, began working on new legislation to control better the flow of refugee claimants into Canada.

The opportunity to push legislative revisions through Parliament came after two ships, one of Tamils in 1986 and another of Sikhs in 1987, illegally landed their respective human cargoes on Canada's East Coast in the dead of night. As the media hinted that more ships were on their way to Canada to deposit additional refugee claimants on Canadian beaches, the government declared an emergency. Despite the protests of pro-refugee advocates, Parliament was recalled and waiting legislation was rushed through to tighten up refugee regulations and impose sanctions on those who aided or abetted the entry of persons to make refugee claims. It was now more difficult for individuals to make a successful refugee claim from within Canada.

In December 1989, as this debate continued, Faduma Abdi arrived in Canada with two of her five children and pregnant with another. She applied for refugee status. Could it be that Canadians wanted to close the door against her and those like her? One can only hope not. Faduma Abdi is from Somalia. She comes from an urban background. University educated and working as a public servant in Mogadishu where she lived with her husband and children, Faduma also volunteered her time to social agencies that assisted dispossessed refugees from Ethiopia who sought refuge in Somalia. Little did she know she would soon be a refugee herself.

In 1986, civil war erupted in Somalia. Later, Faduma Abdi's husband Yusuf Abdi, a political opponent of the ruling regime, was abducted and imprisoned. The army ransacked their home and threatened family members. Faduma fled to the countryside to find refuge for herself and her children. With the help of influential friends and family, her husband was released from detention. Scarred by his prison experience, he managed to secure an escape for his wife and the two youngest children to the United States in December 1989. When he followed by boat with the three remaining children via Kenya, their vessel capsized and he was drowned. Faduma, meanwhile, had made her way to the United States and later to Canada where she applied for status as a Convention refugee. Unknown to Faduma, who feared that her husband had perished with the three children, her two daughters and only son had in fact survived and been sent to a refugee camp in Kenya. Shortly thereafter, she learned that the children for whom she grieved were still alive. The family was reunited in Canada in 1991.

Faduma and her children join an estimated 500,000 refugees whom Canada has admitted since the end of World War II, but will this asylum be available to others who might be threatened in the future? The signals are mixed. In these difficult political and economic times, it will take a particularly strong commitment to human decency for Canadians to withstand mounting pressures to exclude those in need. And there can be no mistake that Canada's refugee protection process has been questioned.

In 1992, the government introduced revisions of the Immigration Act that were designed to make it more difficult for those who wish to make a refugee claim within Canada. Some of these revisions went well beyond what many felt was either necessary or appropriate to process the flow of asylum seekers more effectively. Pro-refugee lobbyists prodded the government into withdrawing several of the more draconian provisions of its proposed legislation, but the essential features of the package passed through Parliament in December 1992. Since then the Canadian government has made it still more difficult for refugees to reach Canada's shores.

The majority of refugees in the world today will eventually be resettled in their countries of origin, but not all of them can be or will be. Since we as Canadians all share in the lives of those who came to Canada as refugees in this generation or generations past, dare we as a nation turn our back on those who still need or will need Canada as a safe haven? It would be a sad commentary on our past and a poor legacy to leave our children if Canada were to lead an international retreat from caring. Surely all those who rejoice that in Canada R 5001 3210 could again be Pham, Thê Trung will not deny Canada to others.

Harold Troper
Ontario Institute for Studies in Education

Czechs/Slovaks

The Straznicky Family

Eva Marha

On 21 August 1968, just over a quarter of a century ago, the Warsaw Pact troops led by the Soviet Union invaded the former Czechoslovakia. For Czechoslovak citizens, this meant that their political and economic future would be rigidly controlled once again by the communists. This loss of freedom was something that many would not tolerate a second time. As a result, thousands of individuals and families of Czech and Slovak origin fled their native country in search of a better life. The reasons for the Straznickys' flight are typical of many of the 1968 and 1969 refugees, yet their story is unique.

Ivan and Marta Straznicky are of Slovak and Czech origins. In the region of Moravia, in Zlín and then Litovel, the family led a typical small-town life with five children in a small apartment and a constant struggle with chronic food shortages. While Ivan worked as a patents officer, much of Marta's day was spent in line-ups, waiting to buy food. ˙

The Soviet-led invasion meant that one could no longer speak or act freely. For the Straznickys, the invasion was a shock. Of course they had heard about what was happening in Prague on the radio, but it did not seem real until a few days later when they encountered tanks on their way to church. They were frightened and realized for the first time that the recently gained freedom of the Prague Spring was gone when they heard the rumble of the tanks while people were singing the national anthem inside the church.

Although daily life did not change noticeably after the invasion, they had intense fear for the future under communism.

Ivan's father had spent ten years in a communist concentration camp, and the family never recovered. His family was blacklisted. One result was that he was never allowed to study at a university. Ivan was convinced that their children's fate would be the same. In addition, the Straznickys were devout Catholics. After the invasion, Christian churches stayed open, but once again churchgoers were not regarded favourably.

At the time of the Prague Spring, Ivan and Marta had five children, ranging in age from two to nine, and Marta was pregnant. Making the decision to leave was difficult. After the invasion of Prague, Ivan knew that they must act quickly while the borders were still open. The pregnant Marta was simply afraid to pack up and go to an unfamiliar place with five young children. The thought of leaving both sets of grandparents behind was devastating, but the spectre of staying in Czechoslovakia with the knowledge that their children would have no future was even worse.

Ivan used a business trip to England in 1969 as an opportunity to call his pen-pal in France, who was keeping in touch with the Canadian embassy in Paris, to arrange the family's escape. With the Czechoslovakian borders still open, the major problem in leaving was registering all five children in the parents' passports. At least one or more of the children had to remain as insurance that the family would return. Fortunately, officials were confused and, thanks to bureaucratic bungling, they were allowed to leave with all five children. As arranged, they sought asylum at the Canadian embassy in Paris.

They arrived in Ottawa on 20 March 1969. The Department of Manpower and Immigration arranged hotel accommodations for them. They received free basic household necessities from the government and non-profit organizations, but the family had to repay a loan that was given to them for the air transportation from France to Canada.

Initially, the family had only $25 to live on. Ivan managed to find a job after two weeks, albeit far below his professional qualifications, but it allowed the family to move to their own home. Over the years, the Straznickys have helped a number of other Czech and Slovak refugees through the local chapter of the Czechoslovak Association of Canada.

The Straznickys retain their language and some customs. The children are all able to understand and communicate in Czech. Some of the children have married into Canadian families and all have finished high school; some have gone on to university. Lenka, who was nine when they came, lives in Ottawa, is married, and has two children. Michal, who came to Canada when he was eight, also lives in Ottawa, is married, has one child, and works as a phone mechanic for Bell Canada. Marta, who was seven, is now a professor of English at Queen's University in Kingston and is also married. Ivan, who was five, works for a consulting firm in Toronto. Magdalene, who was two, is a chartered accountant in Ottawa and is married. John, who was born here, has recently left the University of Ottawa to work in Toronto. David, who was also born here, still lives at home and studies economics at Carleton University.

The Straznickys have no regrets about their decision to leave the former Czechoslovakia. They feel that although they can visit the newly independent and democratic Czech Republic now almost once a year, Canada is their home.

The Straznicky Family Speaks

Interviewed by Eva Marha

Ivan I was born in Slovakia, in the village of Zvolenská Slatina, which is in central Slovakia. Perhaps I should explain that my grandmother lived there. At the time of my birth, we lived in Bzenec, in southern Moravia. It was the tradition in my mother's family that the daughters would come back home and give birth to the children at the place where they were born. My mother went there for my birth and my sisters' births.

My nationality is Canadian now, but I am half Czech and half Slovak. My mother comes from a Slovak family and she was born in Slovakia. She attended schools in Slovakia and went to a convent school in Liberec, in northern Bohemia. And my father, typically Czech, was born in Vienna. I have a Czech education and am a citizen of the Czech Republic, as I found out about two years ago, to my surprise. Later, under the new Czech Citizenship Act, I became a citizen of Slovakia. Change is life.

Marta My background is simpler than his. I was born in Zlín. It was renamed Gottwaldov during the communist regime. Now again it is Zlín. And I am Czech.

Ivan My father had a drugstore in the small Moravian town of Bzenec. It is a wine-growing region. During the crisis in the thirties, he went bankrupt. He then applied for a job in Zlín at Bata, the shoemakers. He became a manager in a huge department store's electrical appliance department, so we moved from southern Moravia to central-eastern Moravia.

I received my education in Zlín. We also lived for seven years in Litovel, which is in northern Moravia. We moved there because we could not get an apartment in Zlín at that time–there was a shortage of apartments. A company in Litovel offered me a position and a company apartment–that's why we moved there.

Marta I lived in Zlín until we married. There was a real shortage of housing in communist Czechoslovakia. We lived in my parents' house and later at his mother's place. And then we got an apartment in Litovel, another town, and he got a job there. Four of our children were born in Zlín. And the last child born in Czechoslovakia was born in Olomouc because the maternity hospital was there. Litovel was a small town of 5,000 to 8,000 people, so there was no hospital there, only a health clinic.

Ivan The first time that we went there, we went by train. Zlín, where we grew up, is surrounded by mountains. Litovel is just flat. There was a cemetery in Litovel and I used to say to myself "I hope that this is not the cemetery where I am going to be buried." We moved there after much hesitation only because there was no hope of getting an apartment in Zlín. There I worked for a research institute in a patent department. We had been promised that they would allocate us an apartment, but when one became available, they said, "Later, later, later." There always happened to be a member of the Communist party who got the priority. So eventually we decided that we had to go and we went, but we never called Litovel home, really. We felt at home in Zlín. With a friend of ours who lived in the same apartment as we did in Litovel, we purchased one of the cottages from the exhibition in Olomouc. It was one of the great worldly possessions for us. We moved it to the Jeseník mountains in northern Moravia shortly before we left.

We had four children then. Our third child was born shortly before we moved to Litovel. And then we had two more children in Litovel, so we did not have money flowing out of our ears.

I used to play competitive volleyball in Zlín. In Zlín, I also passed a state exam in English, which qualified me to teach evening courses for beginners in English. And I also did some freelance translating.

Marta   With five small children, I didn't have enough time to become involved in any kind of activities in the community. Ivan was thirty-six and I was thirty-three. The children were nine, eight, seven, five, and two, and I was pregnant. I was a home-maker. I had worked as a secretary in Zlín when we got married in 1959 before we had the children. But after the first child was born, that was it, because the children were born one after the other.

Ivan   One of the terrible things in that country for me was the working hours because it started at six o'clock in the morning. I'd get up around five-thirty, maybe later. Since I had to serve in the army, of course I learned to eat and dress fast, so I'd throw everything in as quickly as I could. Then I'd go to work, which was about a seven-minute walk or a three-minute run. I had to run because one of the most important aspects of a good employee then was never being late. I would be there at one minute before six, sometimes one minute after six so I had to make excuses as to why I was late. And I joined the crowds who were doing the same thing, running to be there on time and punching the clock. I was in charge of the patent department and the technical information department library. There were two people there. So the daily routine would be that of a patent agent, plus some management, maybe some meetings with the research and development people of the company and from other firms. The day would end at two o'clock.

I would come home and have a little nap because I had to get up so early in the morning and then we would go for a walk with the children, depending on the time of year. We used to play recreational volleyball. We would take the children to a place where other friends gathered and play volleyball there.

We had a little garden lot in the suburbs. With so many children, there were lots of activities at home. The children had homework and so on. In the evening we would have supper and I would read them a story or two.

Marta Just preparing them for sleep took at least one hour. The evening was the busiest time of the day in our place.

Ivan And we had to wash the diapers, of course. There were no disposables then. We were ozone friendly. We were really busy with raising the children. There was a shortage of virtually everything.

Marta My routine was getting up in the morning after he left and preparing the older kids for school. Going shopping was very time-consuming. You didn't shop for the whole week–you shopped for the day, and you didn't know what you were going to cook because you didn't know what you were going to get. There were lines in front of every store, especially if they got something that was in shortage–from oranges to wieners to meat, even butter sometimes. There was a shortage of lots of things, especially in the small towns. I remember when Ivan went for a business trip to Prague, I would give him money to buy butter. All I could get in our town was a quarter pound of butter *osminka*. A quarter-pound of butter for one week.

Ivan That's what you got. There was no rationing, of course, but that's all that they could give you. When your turn came up in the store, "There's your quarter-pound, goodbye."

Marta Meat was in very big shortage. Lunch in Czechoslovakia is like supper here. We had lunch with the children because they had school from eight till one. In the afternoon, we would help them with homework and piano lessons.

Ivan On the weekends, we would sometimes travel, by train or by bus. Sometimes we would go to visit our children's grandparents in Zlín. Sometimes they would come visit us. The routine included church, and that was about it. We didn't have a car. That was a luxury beyond our means then, even though later we started saving money for a car.

Marta About 90 per cent of the women I knew in our neighbourhood in Litovel were working outside the home. I was an exception because one child came after the other and I didn't have time to go to work.

Ivan I came from a family of four children. My father was well-to-do. Even though my mother was educated and had some kind of junior degree that authorized her to work in drugstores, she stayed home with us. My father was arrested by the communists in 1950 and taken from his office. It took two and a half years for us to find out what he was charged with. I was sixteen years old then. We were left completely without any means, so my mother had to go to work. The labour market was state-controlled. The only job she could get was doing hospital laundry for a pittance, even though she was qualified to work in a more responsible and better-paid position. With her husband being an enemy of the state, she and all of us were automatically enemies also, you see.

Eventually my father went to the state court and was accused of sabotaging something, but the court proceedings were about what he had to say while in jail. It was a terrible experience, certainly enough to make you withstand any hardship in exile. My father was taller than I am and he was a stocky man. When we saw him at court after two and a half years, he looked like the corpses you can see in photos from the Nazi concentration camps. My sister fainted when he walked in, and there were all kinds of things that I don't like to talk about. To make a long story short, he was not politically involved in any way. He was against communism, but he was not an active anticommunist. When we talked about it later, we felt that there must have been someone who wanted his job and they just used this to get the job. He spent ten years in concentration camps all across the country.

In communist concentration camps in Czechoslovakia, people usually worked in mines. There were uranium mines in western Bohemia. My father was there. He was also in eastern Bohemia where the coal mines were. We visited him there after he was sentenced. There were towers, dogs, guards, and everything, like a clipping from the Nazi camps.

During the Prague Spring era, I was approached by some fellow workers in my company who requested that I represent their group in the labour union movement. I was not a member of the Communist party ever. When the Soviets invaded us, I knew that the situation was going to get worse, and I did not want to live there. Whether I would have been sent to jail or a concentration camp, I don't know. Maybe not, maybe yes. I would have lost my job for sure, as I had been actively involved in discussions and the union activities during that brief period of freedom in 1968.

My fondest memories go back to my childhood. They are of the summer holidays at my grandmother's in Slovakia. My grandparents owned a cheese factory. There were eighteen cousins. My grandmother took care of us during the summer. That was fun. When you are young, you are fond of many other things, of course. Later, I used to play competitive volleyball and we would travel with the team, but not abroad.

I remember when the Soviets invaded in 1968. There was a huge crowd around the company director's car at the factory gate. The radio was blasting in the car with the news. We just didn't believe that it had happened. In hindsight, it was bound to happen. I personally didn't believe it would happen because it didn't make too much sense for the Soviets to come. I was shocked and saddened because I had already made some arrangements with the company to start my own business–all those things were gone. The shock and anger are difficult to describe now.

Marta I had the same disbelief. We thought it was almost impossible. And when it happened, it was so bizarre, we were in shock.

Ivan A friend of mine was one of the people manning a radio station, and it worked for more than one month after the invasion. They were moving from one place to another, broadcasting news about the moves of the Soviets.

Marta At that time, the twenty-second of August, I was at my mother's place in Zlín, with the children, just to visit. I saw the tanks. When I went to church, the tanks were coming or going on the main street. That was bizarre because everything was peaceful and nobody was shooting. In every tank, you could see the head of a soldier with a helmet. It was like a movie, not like real life. After church, we sang a Czech hymn, and everybody was in tears. You could hear the tanks from the church.

Ivan There was an organ blasting in the church, people singing the national anthem, and the clatter of the Soviet tanks in the background. Things like that give you shivers.

The Soviets did not close the churches down. You could still go to church and we used to go to church. Before the Soviets came, religion was officially prohibited. If you sent your children to Sunday religion classes, they would not be allowed to go to university. There were religion classes outside of school. That was the case with my nieces, who had tried for several years before they got to university.

We were a big family. There were very few families with that many children, one or two children was the norm for a long time before us. Soviet invasion or not, the children were small and we had to bathe them in the evenings, tell them stories, and take them for a walk. The routine did not change much immediately after the Soviet invasion, but what did change was the fear of things to come because there was no doubt that things were going back to the hard-line communist days.

I still have a letter here from the 1950s from the Slovak Ministry of Education explaining that even though I had passed the admission exam to the university, they could not admit me because my father had spent time in a concentration camp. So communism, or socialism as they called it, to me is bad thing–to put it very mildly.

I would have emigrated from communist Czechoslovakia ten years earlier at least if I could have, but before 1968 the border was sealed–there were fences, watch-towers, mines, dogs–you name it–and you couldn't go. When the Soviets came, I began thinking immediately about leaving the country. It didn't make sense for me to stay because I would be persecuted again. There were some things said during Prague Spring that some people remembered–you know revenge was to be expected.

Emigrating from the country was the only solution. I knew that my kids would not be able to go to the university, if for no other reason than because we were churchgoers. I am not a religious fanatic, but going to church is important to me and I was not prepared to give that up.

I knew that the children would suffer because of that. I had a reasonably good job, good income. My standing there as a professional was much higher than it was in Canada after we moved, but we were beginning to talk about emigration.

Marta   Ivan started to talk about our emigration. It was the beginning of September 1968. I said "No way," because I was really afraid– scared to death to leave my nicely furnished apartment. Ivan gave me reasons why we should leave. And I gave him my reasons why we should stay home.

Ivan   There were many families in which the man would emigrate first, leaving the wife behind, expecting to bring the wife and children later. And there were married couples who left children behind with grandparents. I felt very strongly that I would not leave without the whole family in one group. This was one of the questions posed to me at the Canadian embassy in Paris, when I was interviewed for my landed immigrant status. I thought the family must go together. To me, if I could not persuade my wife that we should leave, then we would not have a good chance of starting anew. Of course, everybody knew that it would be a hard life at the outset. We certainly didn't come here to have it better economically. That was not a consideration at that time.

Marta We told the children we were going to France for recreation.

Ivan I had a pen-pal for seventeen years. We had never met. Her name is Odette, and she is French.

Before the Prague Spring, you simply couldn't go abroad if the Communist party did not allow you to. After the Prague Spring, anybody could go. And certainly, shortly after the invasion, the Czechoslovakian authorities would let anybody go if you had a piece of paper that said somebody was going to pay for your stay abroad. There was no convertibility between the currencies, so even though by 1968 we had enough money in Czechoslovakian currency, it was no use to us abroad. So I just wrote my pen-pal that she had to invite us, and she did. We were still afraid to put all of our children in our passport applications. We made two trips. The second time, we emigrated. The first time we went just to persuade my wife that life would be better in the West than it is in the communist regime.

Marta We were invited to go to France at the beginning of December for one week or ten days and we went there with three children. Two children were staying with my mother.

Ivan We were undecided as to whether we wanted to emigrate to New Zealand, Australia, or Canada. I didn't want to go to their embassies in Prague because I knew, obviously, that they must be under surveillance already, so I wanted to go to Paris to visit the embassies there and then see what would happen.

Marta It was very hard for me to leave. You are attached to even material things plus, of course, family, parents, surroundings, and everything. I felt miserable at that time because I did not know English and I was pregnant.

Ivan I don't think that you should have the impression that we left the country without a consensus. There was consensus. Before I left for work in the morning, we would discuss it and decide that we were going, but by the afternoon, my wife, being pregnant, got tired and had different thoughts, and we were not going. The next morning we were going and the next afternoon we weren't going. It went on like this for some time. One afternoon when, again, we were not going, I asked her if she knew what she wanted. She said that she did not, and I said that if she did not, then I did. We were going, and she said "Okay." And we went.

Marta He decided and I just followed him. I could not decide on my own. It was a struggle every day because I thought it was the biggest decision of my whole life. When he decided and I said okay, it was easier for me. I was relieved because he knew English. I knew he was going to do something about our well-being. I trusted him and it was easier.

Ivan We flew to Paris. I was making a very good income because I had a good knowledge of the classification of American patents. I made good extra money with my expertise, so it was no problem for us to buy tickets to Paris as long as you were purchasing them in Czechoslovakia.

I organized the first trip as a sightseeing tour for her to see life in the West. I was hoping that when she saw that you don't have to stand in a line-up at the butcher's every day, that you can go to the market and they have fish if you want it, and if you wanted to buy a kilo of butter, it is there to buy. I was hoping that she would agree that we were going.

Marta It was absolutely terrific in France. I liked it very much. When we came home from Prague by train to the city of Olomouc, it was absolutely dark, and at every corner there was a Soviet soldier. I said to myself that I was going to leave. It was like the Middle Ages, like a nightmare. Comparing those two countries, France and Czechoslovakia, worked for me, but unfortunately, just for a couple of days. Then I settled into my routine. Staying with our friend was more like being tourists than refugees. We didn't really know what it would be like to be an immigrant or a refugee there. It was not going to be easy. And again I said, "No," to him because I thought it would be hard, very hard with those small children. I couldn't provide more money for the family. I knew that. It was as if my hands were tied, and maybe that's why I was afraid to go. I knew I could not work, that somebody must be with the children. It would all be on him.

Ivan We visited the three embassies and chose Canada strictly on superficial things. We chose Canada because of the way we were treated at the embassy. With the Australians and New Zealanders, you had the impression that they thought you might be allowed to come to that country. But in the Canadian embassy, there were no reservations–"Of course, come over. No problem. Welcome."

We wanted to get the remaining two children on our application forms. We communicated with my pen-pal in code, that she had a rich mother in the French Alps with a resort, who would invite us for the winter holidays. The rich mother was Canada, and the resort, of course. We have been in the resort ever since.

Marta Then in January 1969, he was sent on a business trip to England.

Ivan I had to go on the business trip. It was a total surprise. Before 1968, I really wanted to go, but only the communists were allowed then. I was in London with another guy, who didn't know what was going on. At night when he fell asleep, I ran downstairs and spent most of my money calling my friend in Paris, trying to explain that we'd be there as soon as possible.

Marta He came back from England and said, "Either we go right now or we are staying." My heart just stopped beating because I knew the time was very near. I had to go to the town hall to register my children in the passport–the remaining two because they had not been in France. The official asked me what the purpose of the trip was, and I said recreational. The smallest one, Magdalene, was two years old. He pointed at her and said, "You are leaving her here at home as security, aren't you?" But at the same time, he was writing her name in the passport.

Ivan It paid to have more children in a situation like that. He was totally confused. He saw two or three children and he put two of them in the application, not realizing that the other two children were in my passport, not in hers.

Marta It was quite hard to say goodbye to our parents because at that time we thought we weren't going to see each other again.

Ivan The choice was made between your children and your parents. You had to make that choice. If you chose your parents, your children's future could be in jeopardy. And if you chose your children, then your parents were the ones to suffer.

Marta It was hard for us, but it was harder for them. It was not only us, their grandchildren were leaving too.

Ivan We flew to Paris again. The second day in Paris, I went to the Canadian embassy, but they couldn't find the file from our first interviews there. I was interviewed by an RCMP guy who was just nasty with me. He was asking why I went to England if I wanted to emigrate. If I was here in December, why did I go back? I told him it was because we had two children back there. He said there are many families who leave their family behind. I said I would not come without my children.

The day after, the immigration counsellor at the embassy, Mr Raymond, who had interviewed me the first time in December, phoned my pen-pal, Odette, at work apologizing for the mix-up. She made arrangements for another interview and I went to the embassy again, this time to Mr Raymond. He said that everything was all right–we went through medical exams and other formalities. He asked when we wanted to leave and we said, "Tomorrow." He said, "Well, not tomorrow, but we can book you for the day after tomorrow." So we left the day after tomorrow. We spent one week in Paris, something totally unbelievable to those who tried later. We had five children–or five and a half–but somehow it was relatively easy. We did not have to spend lots of time in camps. We were scared of that and were grateful for the speedy processing, of course.

In fact, we were never afraid that we might be turned down by the Canadian authorities. It never crossed my mind. Yet, as we were leaving for Canada from France, we still had about two days left on our exit visas issued by the Czech government, so we could have gone back and no one would have known. We had a few possessions that we hoped we could sell, if worse came to worse.

While in France, we stayed in La Garenne-Colombes, which is about 50 km northwest of Paris, in my pen-pal's house. She was married and they had two children and a nanny. They took good care of us. The nanny was from Montreal.

We stayed for seven days. We were at the embassy three times for medicals and everything for the remaining two children. The other three children had already passed the medical the first time we were there.

Life at our friends' house was relatively comfortable, as much as it could be. We invaded their house. There were lots of us. We stayed in two rooms. Our children were very well behaved. When

Odette later came to visit us in Canada, she still remembered how well behaved our kids were. While in France, we still hadn't told the children because we realized that we might have to go back. We didn't want the children to go back to school and talk because that might mean jail for us–you never know, so we didn't tell them. They didn't know what was going on and they thought we were on holiday. And then when all was done and signed and sealed, we told them.

Marta We told them that we were not going back to Czechoslovakia. We were going to Canada, forever. Their reaction was, "Hooray." They were absolutely amazed that we were going to a distant place. But Lenka, the oldest, started to think about it and questioned us. She said, "Well, how about my teacher? How about Grandma? How about my best friend?" That was her reaction after the big hooray. The rest of the children–Michal, Ivan, and Magdalene–didn't think that something would happen to Grandma. We said that we were going to write a letter to her teacher and explain everything, and to Grandma, and to her best friend, and then she was all right. Which is what we did, actually. Yes, we wrote a couple of letters to Ivan's company and co-workers to tell them that we weren't coming back.

Ivan We were government-sponsored in Canada. That's why I say it was much easier for us than for people before and after us. The sponsorship program was in place and the clearance was fast. I understand that unlike in the United States, in Canada, members of the Communist party could come as long as they did not lie about their membership. I was told this by the RCMP guy, who, I suspect, must have thought that I was lying to him about my past. In retrospect, even with the RCMP episode, it was all very easy. When we arrived in Canada, we were classified as landed immigrants. At the time, I knew that there were lakes in Canada. But I didn't expect that when you look at the map of northern Ontario, it looks like Finland. So many lakes–it just resembled

Finland to my recollection of geography. I knew that the patent office was here in Ottawa. I was a patent agent and I wanted to continue my profession here, so I asked to be sent to Ottawa for that reason. And this is where we have stayed ever since.

Marta My knowledge about Canada was poor. I thought that winter here was 365 days. And our first summer–it was 1969–was very hot. I couldn't believe that in Canada you could have such a hot and humid summer. I wrote to my mother asking her to send us swimsuits. They came in time, just before the summer. The kids could go and swim.

Ivan We didn't have money to buy the kids swimsuits then.

Marta There was no way because we had $25 a week for everything, which was nothing, even at that time. We didn't have enough money for haircuts.

Ivan I used to speak with different people in Czechoslovakia about Canada. I even asked people in England during that business trip. And they would say, "Oh, the Americans are noisy." I would ask, well, what about the Canadians? And they would just look at me and say the same thing. So basically when you come from Europe, I don't think you see much difference, but I have to qualify that by saying that I never lived in the United States. We never considered immigration to the United States. I don't know why. I didn't have a particular reason. It just didn't occur to me. The preoccupation then was to get out of the region away from the damn Russians. That was what mattered. Where you went was secondary in a way.

Marta You were not thinking about the nice weather just to get out. I wanted to go to New Zealand because I read an article that in New Zealand there were no snakes. We flew to Montreal and from Montreal to Ottawa. It was arranged in Paris that someone would be waiting for us. Slowly but surely, the people disappeared, and the Ottawa airport hall was empty except for us. People went home, but our family stayed there waiting for someone to approach us.

Ivan At the time, the Ottawa airport after nine o' clock was totally deserted. You are almost scared there. There was just us with two suitcases and five children, each child holding a doll and what not. We were tired and jet-lagged. Imagine the children. For them, it was four o'clock in the morning. And, of course, Ivan Junior was crying.

I went to a commissioner there, but it was very late at night and he couldn't reach people in the immigration office. We didn't have any money except about $20 we had received at Dorval airport. They were waiting for us in Dorval, everything clicked in Dorval–it was perfect. They knew about us and knew we were coming. "Landed" was stamped in our papers and our transfer plane was there, so we transferred and then we got to Ottawa and no one was there. We were supposed to go right home. Well, we didn't know where we were supposed to go.

Marta The kids were sitting on the suitcases. That commissioner had a very hard time because he knew that there was a family and no one was coming for us. Then finally after one hour of phoning and phoning, he reached somebody at home. A lady came to the airport with her arms opened wide and she said "Welcome to Canada"–after we had been in Canada for eighty-eight hours. She came with a taxi and took us to the Alexandra Hotel, which no longer exists. She gave us instructions about what to do in the morning. We would have breakfast and show up at Manpower. After that, it was very well organized. In the morning, I peeked through the blinds in the hotel room and all I could see was a recently burnt house on Bank Street.

Ivan There was a fire across the street the night before. We opened the blinds, we looked at Bank Street, and there was a burnt-out house. Then you realized the homes were wooden. It was like looking at the scenery from one of those western movies–narrow street with wooden homes. It was not a nice sight.

Marta   No, I didn't like it, especially Bank Street. I think it has changed a lot for the better. It is different now, of course. There is a shopping mall, but twenty-four years ago, it looked like the Wild West to me.

Ivan   Well, we looked at it and that was our impression–we didn't like it. But the main concern was finding a job, so I went to the Manpower office. And there were the children to think of. We went for walks with the children and to church on Sunday. We stayed in the hotel for about two weeks.

Life went on whether you liked it or not. There was no way for us to go back. We could not go back–you don't even think that–so whether you like it or not, this is the choice you made and there is not too much sense in looking back. You just look ahead, find a job. It took me three days to find the patent office. There was a daily routine that was established towards finding a job.

Marta   We came on 20 March–it is the most terrible month here. There was still a little bit of snow on the ground, but it rained and the trees were not green yet, of course.

Ivan   But those are things that you only realize afterwards. When we arrived, you concentrate on what you do–like "today I am going to the Manpower office." I found out very soon that the Manpower office was not going to help me because they were good at finding jobs for blue-collar workers, but had no experience with professional positions.

We were more or less curious to find out what Canada was going to be like. The real surprise to me was the summer–hot, sticky, humid weather. I didn't realize it could be so hot so far up north. The surprises, the unusual things that happened to us were extremely pleasant.

Marta Like lots of groceries in the stores. Wow! You can buy lentils, you can buy oranges.

Ivan We did not have money to buy many things, but that did not matter too much because it just pointed out the sense in trying to work and to do something to make a good income so that I can afford those things later on.

I got a job after two weeks. It was not well paid—it was with the same firm that I am still with. It was in a somewhat different field because I didn't have my professional exam then. When I got my job and I knew how much I would be making, we went looking for an apartment. We went to Bayshore here in Ottawa, which is a complex of townhouses and apartments. They would not let us in because we had too many children—the apartment was too small for us. They offered us a house with more bedrooms, but we couldn't go there.

Eventually we went to an apartment that we could not really afford at the time. It was a townhouse. I wanted to make sure that the overall environment was as good or better than it was in Czechoslovakia. We realized there was not going to be any holiday for the first summer at least. There happened to be a swimming pool in the development, and that was another reason for moving in. There was a nice park, you could see the groomed grass and everything. It looked like luxury to us.

Marta We didn't regret that move.

Ivan We did not have enough money for many things we could have afforded if we had moved into something less expensive. What we could afford on my salary at that time would not be as good as what we had in Czechoslovakia. The aim was to make the living quarters equal to or better than the old ones, and we succeeded in that. It was a hard life at the beginning because we–Marta in particular–had to get by on a shoestring budget, and the string was very, very thin. We didn't have a car for a year. We wanted to save more money for housing.

Marta   The first shopping trip was when I realized it was going to be very tough. We had to be very careful with money.

Ivan   I had to go with the children to introduce them to the school. School was a disappointment. I knew that my son Michal always had problems in math. I met the teacher at the first interview and asked how I could help because Michal has problems with math. "Oh no, he has absolutely no problems." She was very happy to have Michal in her class and had no problems with him. You just leave him alone and let Michal do his thing.

Then we realized that the school system was totally inadequate for true education. It was just a place to have fun and nothing else unless the student really tried on his or her own. To this day, I don't think highly of the Canadian school system.

Marta   Schooling in Canada would be another interview.

Ivan   We had friends here from Litovel, but they didn't live in the same neighbourhood. They didn't know we were coming and we surprised them. They were our former neighbours. We knew about other Czech families, of course, through the grapevine.

Marta   We socialized with Czech people, but because he knew English, we also socialized with Canadians. It was half and half.

Ivan   In the townhouse, the neighbours were curious about us and they would come in and the children brought in their friends after school, so the integration was very easy.

Marta   When the phone rang, it was the most terrible thing to happen for me because the children were either out or at school and he was at work and I had to answer that stupid phone. Immediately I started perspiring. In the beginning I didn't know what people were talking about on the phone. I just listened and I had one statement: "I'm sorry, I cannot speak English. Can you please phone later?" or something like that. A few phrases. And when people come to sell things, that was something else too. I would open the door and the guy would talk to me, "blah blah blah." I did not understand. Once I said, "No money, you know," and he said "Oh, I know," and he left. Ever since, when someone in our family says "No money, you know," it means go away.

I went to English classes twice a week for not even a year because I got pregnant again with the youngest one, David. I had to stop. I did not go back after he was born. Finally I just learned English from the people outside and from my kids because they started to speak English half a year after we came. They started to talk English at home. It took me almost five to seven years to learn English. I learned from experience, not from school.

Ivan   I certainly found things very different, but I did not expect to find them the same. I never thought of the degree or difference with this or that. I didn't have any problem adjusting. When John was born, we had a Canadian godmother and a Canadian godfather from our church. We had neighbours there. We were surprised to see how many people owned their own homes. We saw that the homes weren't as posh or as expensive as the homes in Europe, but they had their own homes and their privacy.

Before I started looking for a job, I went to the barber's in the hotel we stayed at. The barber was Dutch and we began talking about this and that. He said that I will like it here, and I heard the same thing from a Hungarian immigrant on the plane coming over here.

Even though I had not been exposed to English that much prior to coming here–it was mainly listening to the radio and I had been in England for those two weeks–I noticed that people had different accents.

And everybody was nice. Once, we were walking home from church and there was a dog running out of a house to our children. A lady came out from the house and she noticed we were talking in a strange language. She asked where we were from and she said, "I hope you will like it in Canada." Things like that did not happen to you in Czechoslovakia in those days.

Marta We were sensitive that we might be noticed more because of those details.

Ivan Something like that makes your day, and that's what I consider Canadian culture. You know, nice people, understanding, willing to help, and we have been trying to do the same thing.

I know people who came here, Czech and Slovaks for instance, who could not live with the thought that they had left behind their curtains. "I had such a nice set of curtains there and it is all left behind with the furniture and everything." The furniture we had here at the beginning was terrible by our standards from Europe, but it was all temporary. We came here to start a new life, and for a new life, it was not all that bad.

Our first flatware was not even stainless steel. In our beds, we had bedbugs.

Marta We got mattresses with bedbugs. That was terrible.

Ivan We didn't like that. It was terrible. It was painful because we got old beds from Neighbourhood Services.

Marta Everything was second-hand. It would have been all right if it was clean.

Ivan That and the language were not a great beginning. The biggest disappointment was the school system. I was shocked by it.

1. Ivan Straznicky with Lenka, Michal, Marta, Ivan, Magdalene, and David (sled), with a friend, on the Rideau Canal, *c.*1971 (Photo: courtesy of the Straznicky family)

2. Ivan and Marta Straznicky with their children. From left: John, Magdalene, Ivan, David, Michal, Lenka, and Marta, *c.*1974 (Photo: courtesy of the Straznicky family)

It is fine if you are selfish, if you have a competitive edge. It took me only that one interview at the school to realize that my children will be the ones taken over by their competitors coming from Asia or you name it because of the poor schooling system, which makes fun the primary objective of the school. We were quite concerned over that. We couldn't even consider sending our children to any private school or anything.

When we came, we received the very basics. That means we had a wooden chair painted in grey for each person in the family, an old table, like an old kitchen table, which was small for the family. Then a couple of beds–the queen size for the children– some linen. But the cutlery was not stainless steel, not even poor quality stainless steel. It was some kind of steel that would rust before you had time to dry it after you washed it.

Marta But that was just temporary. From the Manpower office, we got $60 for the first grocery shopping. They paid the first month's rent for us, and that was about all.

Ivan We had to repay the loan for the air travel. There was interest then, and we chose the lowest payments because that was all I could afford on my salary. We were paying that off for about two years. We had baby bonus, but it was not so much.

I did not have much trouble finding work. As I said, I am a patent agent by profession. I started working as a searcher first, a low-paid job. Then I passed my exam and since I had a reading knowledge of German and Russian, they asked me to manage the foreign department to take care of patent applications abroad.

I felt like a fish in water here. I didn't pass the exam at first because I didn't realize how much of case-law I had to study, but I'd been happy with my work because I could prove my worth.

A few weeks after we moved into our townhouse, I became involved in starting a Czechoslovak weekend school. There were so many new immigrants from Czechoslovakia at that time that there was no problem in finding teachers. We needed two or three teachers, so we got together a group of people who wanted to start the school. Through the Czechoslovak Association, we applied for some help with renting rooms and stuff like that, and we established a school. Then, after several years, we found out that it was in vain because the children were losing the Czech language, which did not make me feel all that bad because we came here to integrate. Then I was no longer involved in the school. I do not personally think that when you come to a new country you should make it one of your important priorities to support the ethnic element of your life. We have Czech friends, Slovak friends, French-Canadian friends, Finnish-Canadian friends, but I never believed in a strong ethnic community life. I can understand that other people may feel otherwise, but I do not feel that way.

At one point, I was approached by the Czechoslovak Association with a request that I join and take care of the program of sponsoring refugees. I'm Christian, so I said that is something to help your neighbour. I accepted and worked for twelve years under the agreement that the Czechoslovak Association made with the federal government in sponsoring refugees from Czechoslovakia. We were trying to raise money from dances and stuff like that for sponsoring families. That didn't work too well, so we then tried to find families who would be willing to shelter new refugees for one year. When we found someone, we would make an agreement with that family so that our obligation to the federal government–accepting financial obligation for the refugee family–would be met by the host family. Of course we had enough money to step in if anything happened. When they arrived here in Ottawa, we would be prepared.

Marta The first question from the refugees, most of whom had spent a long time in European refugee camps, was "We would love to cook dumplings. Where can we find coarse flour for dumplings?" I said forget about that. You can cook very good dumplings from instant flour.

Ivan   And other very basic information, like how the mailbox works, how do you go to the doctor, what do you do with this. We had about ten pages of general information, and met with the refugees. That was my involvement in the community. In 1989 when communism ended, there was no point for me to continue.

I am not a member of the Czechoslovak Association for other reasons. There was a disagreement as to what our approach should be to some people at the postcommunist embassy of Czechoslovakia–that was the basic disagreement. It was a friendly disagreement. I took the position that it was none of our business to tell the Czech government whether they should have this person or that person at the embassy, so that's why I am no longer a member. To be honest, I would not have been a member if it were not for the refugees because that made sense to me. I knew where I could help. I knew the language, I knew the people who needed me, so that was fine with me to organize help.

Despite my low income, one of the first things I did was rent a typewriter. I couldn't buy one, but we rented one and we wrote to our parents. Four pages, single-spaced text of our first impressions every week. We have the first ten years of those letters, and they are very valuable, of course.

Marta   When the postman came, there were usually five or six letters.

Ivan   We wrote friends and friends wrote back to us. The correspondence was there. We were careful because we knew some of the letters were censored, no question about that, but we only reported pleasant things. We didn't write to our parents about the hardship because we didn't want to disturb them.

Marta   The first visitor from the old country was my father in 1972, then my mother. They couldn't come together–they would not let them. Then his mother came in another year, then his father too. Only the parents, not brothers and sisters.

Ivan We found out to our surprise that they spent with us more days per year than when we lived in Litovel only 100 km from them, which of course was natural because they only came for the weekends in Czechoslovakia. They came here sometimes for half a year or three-quarters of a year.

We first went back in May 1990. The second visit there was a business trip in 1990. We organized a seminar about Canadian and US patent law with an associate of mine. And in May we went with the whole family.

Marta No, in 1990 twice, 1991 once, and 1992 twice–five times.

Ivan We resolved to go there every year as long as our mothers were alive because our fathers had died already. Our mothers can't make it here because they are too old.

Marta It was very emotional when we went back for the first time.

Ivan The first time we flew to Amsterdam, rented a car, and drove all the way through Mikulov north of Vienna. At the border, I felt like a little Napoleon because I didn't have to give in and they had to give in. We drove on the highways from Amsterdam to Vienna. Then we went up north and all of a sudden the Austrian villages begin and the highway gets narrower and narrower. And then comes the border with lots of these guys in green uniforms, idling. The watch-tower is still there, but no one was manning it, of course. I don't know if they removed the minefields by then. They probably did.

We drove in the country and it was in total disrepair. It was like after World War II. It was a shock and then the second shock came when we drove in at about five, six, seven o'clock in the evening. It was still light, but it was cold, so people were burning coal in the villages. When we drove by the fields, we could smell the chemicals from the fields. Then we drove into the village and it seemed as if somebody put my head in a bag of flour, stirred the flour and threw in a box of burning matches. I had to breathe that stuff. There was total devastation. The train cars were unbelievably beat up and dirty.

Zlín used to be a garden city and now it was a dirty, smoky place–it made me angry. That was the sad side of it, but the friends were something else. It was an unqualified welcome, even from people who used to be communists. After twenty years, one becomes more tolerant. Maybe Canadian culture makes you acquire tolerance towards many different views even if you may not like them. But it did not feel like home. Home is here–in Canada. I could hardly wait to come back. I don't think I could live again in Europe. I go to Europe on business. Western Europe is in much better shape than the Czech Republic, but our home is here. Our children are here and that probably has something to do with it also, even though it is always pleasant to meet people there.

Marta Yes, we are always in touch with people there by doing tapes, and we go there about twice a year now.

Ivan I try and do a little bit of business. I have ordered there some searching and made arrangements for people to come here and work. I try to help, but I don't look back.

The Czech customs in our family are mainly reflected in the way we celebrate Christmas, which our children always liked, unlike the other things. When we forced them away from the TV, they complained about not being a Canadian family. But on Christmas, our main event takes place on Christmas Eve, not Christmas day, so the children always have their presents half a day earlier than their friends from school.

Marta What we gave up was the celebration of name days.

Ivan We used to celebrate them. We had a good friend named Joseph, and St Joseph's Day is almost worse in Czechoslovakia

than St Patrick's Day. It is a big celebration because every second
person is a Joseph. We gave up Easter Monday customs. It only
lasted five years.

We no longer drink the way we use to. In Czechoslovakia, the
bottle would come on the table and you wouldn't go until the bottle was empty.

Marta When I like food in a restaurant or in another family's
home, I'm not shy to ask for the recipe and try it at home. It
means I can now prepare Lebanese, Mexican, whatever–I don't
even remember–meals.

Ivan Even hamburgers she knows. It took us a long time to get
used to barbecuing, but eventually we couldn't resist.

Marta But you know why? Because we noticed that barbecuing
is a man's job here, and usually it is done outside. Because he is
the man who doesn't like to show that he is doing something, too,
it was the best tactic for a couple of years simply not to buy a
barbecue.

Ivan No comment.

Because of our defection to Canada, the children were de-
prived of seeing their grandparents and family. There are uncles
and other relatives in the old country. We had a family reunion
last year. The whole Canadian family attended except for the two
girls who couldn't go because of work. They all went and they
liked it very much. They now have a feeling of belonging to a
family and are just crazy about getting pictures of the people they
met from the old days, so now the feeling is of belonging to an
even bigger family.

Our oldest daughter has married an English-Canadian, whose
family has been here for ten generations, from Kirkland Lake.
Marta Junior married a guy whose family is half French and half
English-Canadian. In other words, there is no ethnic solidarity in

our family. I would not insist that my children marry guys from Czech families. This is true integration, so our grandchildren are half-and-half.

Marta   It was up to them to choose their partners.

Ivan   I think the selection of the partners from the same ethnic community is by and large made by the parents. I think it is not the choice of the youngsters if you have a typical Italian-Canadian marriage. I think that the father decides who he or she is going to marry. Our children had freedom of choice in this.

Being an ethnic parent is an interesting experience. Your children realize, of course, that you, their parents, have an accent. That you speak differently, and sometimes say funny things because of not having grown up with the language. At the young age, they are ashamed of their parents' English, but around the age of seventeen or eighteen, they begin to realize that there is something here that the others don't have, and they become proud. Our son Michal is a typical example. At the age of fifteen, he would complain, "Why can't we just be a typical Canadian family?" As I said, we prohibited TV during the week at one point, and they were having a hard time adjusting to that. Mike now works as a mechanic for Bell Canada. When he hears anybody speak Polish or Czech or Slovak, he is proud to be able to try to communicate in that language. He soon discovers that he has no Polish! At the family reunion, our children communicated very well with the rest of the family. The two younger children speak just a little bit. They try very hard when they are in the Czech Republic, but they are not nearly as fluent as the older ones.

Marta   Lenka was nine years old when we arrived in Canada. She went through high school, but didn't want to go to university. She just got a job, got married, and is staying at home with two kids.

Lenka is the oldest. Michal went through high school too. He started to attend CEGEP in Hull, but quit after his first or second year and started to work with Bell Canada. He is married and has one infant boy, who was born just two weeks ago. Michal is the second oldest. The third one is Marta, who went through high school and CEGEP. She went to Montreal to Concordia University for two or three years. She got her Master's in English at Concordia, and did her PhD in Ottawa. Now she has a job at Queen's University as an English literature professor and is married and living in Kingston. She has no children yet. Ivan Junior went to CEGEP, then to Montreal to McGill University and got his degree in mechanical engineering. Now he is in Toronto with a consulting engineering firm. Magdalene went to the University of Ottawa, got a degree in accounting, and passed the exam for CA. She works here in Ottawa as a chartered accountant. She is married and has no children. John attended the University of Ottawa and studied economics, but he did not finish his degree because he got a job offer in Toronto. Now he is working in Toronto. He expects to get married this December. And David is still at Carleton University studying economics in his last semester.

In large families, the older ones take care of the younger ones, and because they always talk English, they started to speak English between themselves. So they spoke just very simple sentences in Czech: "What's for supper, Mom?" and "Can I do this? Can I bring a friend?" The rest of the conversation is in English.

Ivan I am also involved in a Czech band. There is a drum, an accordion. You can only join if you don't know how to play your instrument. It is terrible. If you are half deaf, you'd like it. I play the accordion, the king, the bricklayer's piano. We have been meeting once a week for ten years. We have fun. One of us has a farm, and we have the May celebration. We put on costumes that are purported to be from 1848 and do all kinds of crazy things. There is some dancing, singing, sharing jokes and, of course, gossiping.

3. Ivan Straznicky with his youngest grandson, Steven, in the backyard of his home in Gloucester, Ontario, 1993 (Photo: Vincenzo Pietropaolo)

Marta People are invited to go to the band dances. I wonder why people come because the music is so terrible. They say it is because of their enthusiasm, not their playing. They can sense their enthusiasm, and sometimes they sing.

Ivan It sometimes gives me shivers now and then when we play, but it makes life colourful. It is healthy to be ashamed of yourself now and then. Makes you humble.

Marta There were more bands like that from the older generation. We have some of those tapes. I think they have a very good time when they are playing.

Ivan We have a good time.

Marta Most of the people who come to these dances are Czech and Slovak. I guess you have to be one to go.

Ivan I think there are about 1,100 to 1,500 people in the Czech and Slovak community. The Czechoslovak Association is more attractive to the Czechs than to the Slovaks, who have the Slovak League, Slovak ethnic groups, some of which do not even want to have Czechs there. This is not natural to the Czechs and Slovaks of my age. We did not feel too much difference, and we did not think the country should split. You just take it in stride. There is not much that you can do about it and it is not your destiny that has been decided. In unofficial groups like this band and among friends, there is no difference between Czechs and Slovaks.

Marta We have a Czech priest who comes once a month from Montreal. He serves a Czech mass here. A Slovak priest comes from Cambridge every month, too.

Ivan In Canada, I've never faced discrimination, but people imitate my accent. But so what? You just listen to it and it is never

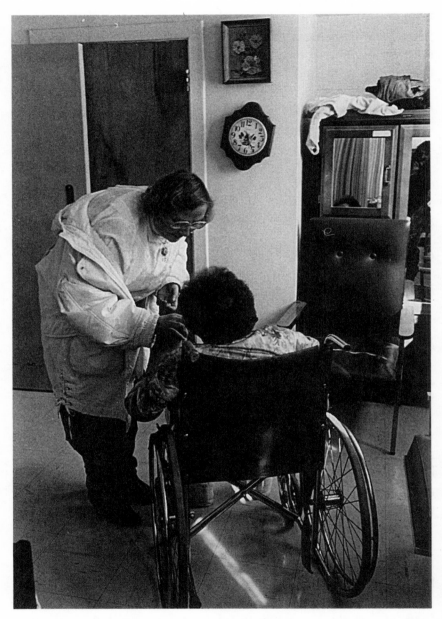

4. Marta Straznicky works as a volunteer at the Madonna Nursing Home for Seniors in Orleans, 1993 (Photo: Vincenzo Pietropaolo)

as bad as listening to your own voice on a tape. You say to yourself, "Is this the way I sound? Well, how terrible!"

To an emigrant, I would certainly recommend Canada over countries like England or Germany, but there has to be a degree of dissatisfaction with the system in your old country. If you are coming only to improve your standard of living, you might be in for a terrible disappointment. And if that is your only aim and you do not make it, then it must be terrible. I know people who are unhappy here or who are homesick. The only homesickness that I ever felt was when I was in Chicago. I could hardly wait to be back in Ottawa. But I've never felt homesick for the old country. I liked the neighbours in the block in the townhouse we first lived in when we moved to Canada. I would recommend Canada as a place to resettle.

I am sure we did the right thing. But I would not do it again now, mind you. One emigration and resettlement is quite enough.

Marta There was no regret really about moving over here.

Ivan I guess if you are a strong family, you can do unbelievable things. I mean survive hardships. And, in our case, we did not mind because there was high hope for something later at the end. In the old country, occupied by the Soviets, dominated by Marxism, there was no future.

Marta This Christmas, Magdalene made a toast and said "Thank you for bringing us here." Things like that give you a true satisfaction and reward for your efforts.

Ivan She was only two years old when we came, but she appreciates being here. She is married to a sixth-generation English-Canadian and is a chartered accountant.

Marta We see the kids about once a month.

5. Ivan and Marta Straznicky at their home in Gloucester, Ontario, 1993
(Photo: Vincenzo Pietropaolo)

Ivan You see, we have many children, so we have many birthdays. They are mostly celebrated here at our house. The children are becoming more generous now and they offer to host some birthdays at their house, which is nice because you do not have to clean the house. But they always do the dishes before leaving for their homes.

Marta We see them at Thanksgiving, Christmas, Easter, plus birthdays and sometimes in between. We visit them also, of course.

Ivan We see our grandchildren and our oldest daughter and her husband almost every week. They stop over on Sunday afternoons, or we will stop over there, or we will join them in skating, camping, or just going to a lake.

I think I would say that we fully appreciate what Canada has done for us, and we are doing our best to return it. It makes me feel good to see that I can contribute to my new country using skills and knowledge, which, in some respects, are new and not widespread here, for instance, classical music.

The Czech/Slovak Community

Eva Marha

Since the establishment of the former Czechoslovak Republic in 1918, there have been four major waves of refugee movements out of the country. The first wave of emigration was driven by economic need, for it was practically impossible for people to find employment during the first few years after the republic was established. During the early 1920s, thousands of people emigrated. Most of them were Slovaks and Carpatho-Rusyns who sought resettlement in the United States. The emigration from Czechoslovakia to Canada in these years was considerably smaller when compared to emigration in the next forty years. In 1922, some 110 people of Czech and Slovak origin emigrated to Canada. In 1923, there were approximately 2,000 to 2,500 emigrants and in 1924 2,800 to 3,100 emigrants.[1]

The next major wave occurred between 1938–39. Czechoslovakia was one of the first targets of Nazi Germany, and the country's Sudeten-German minority provided a good excuse for Hitler's expansion. After Czechoslovakia lost its border regions in September 1938 as a result of the Munich Agreement, the country became completely vulnerable to Hitler's further aggression. In March 1939, Hitler annexed what remained of Bohemia and Moravia and thousands fled the country for political reasons. Most of them were of Jewish origin or communist background.

In 1945, a smaller wave of about 10,000 refugees from Czechoslovakia sought asylum abroad. These people were mostly of Slovak origin, and included former politicians, civil servants, members of the Hlinka Guard, and army officers from the Slovak state, which was allied with Nazi Germany during the war.[2]

A mass exodus started again after the communist coup on 25 February 1948. People fled both harsh economic conditions and political repression, and within a few years some 50,000 Czechoslovakians left the country. Of these, 5,916 emigrated to Canada between April 1947 and December 1951. This new wave of immigrants included a large number of highly qualified people who soon began to participate in Canada's economy and culture.

After the establishment of the communist government in 1948, it soon became practically impossible to flee to the West. In October 1949, four Czechs were sentenced to death for helping people escape, and many others were sentenced to penal servitude for life.[3] This, however, did not discourage any further attempts to flee. Between 1948–49, at least fifty people a day crossed the borders. By 1952, it was reduced to about 100 crossings a month, and during the worst Stalinist times, escape became almost impossible.[4]

The Soviet invasion of Czechoslovakia in August 1968 was a reprisal for the liberalizing reforms of the Dubcek government and gave rise to a larger refugee movement. At the time of the invasion, some 80,000 Czechoslovakian citizens were already abroad. After the invasion, many took advantage of the still-open borders to go abroad as ordinary travellers in order to seek asylum. Many of them chose to wait and see the results. Although in September 1968 the Czechoslovakian government urged its citizens to return, claiming that recent political events posed no threat to them, the number of registrations for emigration abroad increased in the spring of 1969.

On 27 May 1969, the Czechoslovakian government announced an amnesty for all citizens who had left the country illegally after 9 May or whose permits to stay outside the country had expired, if they would return or regularize their status at Czechoslovakian embassies before 15 September 1969. Not many returned. By then, however, there were already some 42,000 Czechoslovakian refugees abroad.[5]

For most, Canada was not a country of first asylum but

served as a resettlement country where refugees could establish new and permanent roots if they chose to do so. Initially, Canada did not take any immediate measures in helping the Czechoslovakian refugees, but by 6 September 1968, Canada was ready to accept them with open arms. According to *The Globe and Mail* (17 September 1968), the Canadian government saw this as an unprecedented opportunity to acquire the most skilled immigrants, including medical doctors, dentists, designers, and electronic and chemical technicians. The Department of Manpower and Immigration set up a special team in Vienna, where most of the refugees were recruited.[6] In all, 11,943 refugees were admitted to Canada between 1968 and 1969.[7]

This group of refugees differed from the 1938 and 1948 groups. It was composed largely of much younger and well-educated people. Many of the refugees also spoke English, French, and German, and they had valid passports and often some financial means. They were mostly students, teachers, scientists, journalists, artists, doctors, and people with other technical and professional skills.[8] Of the 2,643 heads of households who were bound for the Canadian labour market, close to 70 per cent were between the ages of fifteen and forty-four. Nineteen per cent of all the Czechoslovakian refugees who were admitted to Canada in 1968 and 1969 had acquired more than twelve years of formal education, while 33 per cent of the new arrivals were in highly skilled and professional occupational categories. These and other characteristics enabled the Czechoslovakians to integrate quickly in the Canadian economy and society.[9] The total cost to Canadian taxpayers was approximately $11 million, or a little less than $1,000 per refugee. Given their productivity in the Canadian economy, there is little doubt that the return has far outweighed the modest initial investment.[10]

The events of 1968 have in no way stopped the departure of refugees from Czechoslovakia. Although after 1969 it became difficult to leave the country, some 50,000 refugees nevertheless found their way out between 1969 and 1973. It has been estimated that after 1948, about 5,000 refugees a year have managed to flee the country. Canada has continued accepting Czechoslovakian refugees up to the early 1990s. For example, in 1985, 720 Czechoslovakian refugees were admitted to Canada from abroad and in 1986 there were 648 cases. The number of refugees from Czechoslovakia accepted in 1986 is only 3.24 per cent of the total Canadian refugee intake. Between 1978 and 1989, there has also been a small number of Czechoslovakian refugee claimants in Canada. During these twelve years, 282 Czechoslovakians claimed refugee status in Canada.[11] Following the Velvet Revolution of November 1989, the communist government was replaced by a democratic one. Since then, the country has also undergone a voluntary "divorce" to emerge as the Czech Republic and the Republic of Slovakia.

Notes

1. Walter F. Willcox, *International Migrations: Volume I–Statistics* (New York, 1969), pp. 660–61.
2. Paul Tabori, *The Anatomy of Exile: A Semantic and Historical Study* (London, 1972), p. 247.
3. Ibid.
4. Ibid.
5. Louise W. Holborn, *Refugees: A Problem of Our Time: The Work of the United Nations High Commissioner for Refugees, 1951–1972* (Metuchen, N.J., 1975), p. 517.
6. Gerald E. Dirks, *Canada's Refugee Policy: Indifference or Opportunism?* (Montreal, 1977), p. 234.
7. Alan Nash, *International Refugee Pressures and the Canadian Public Policy Response* (Ottawa, 1989), p. 125.
8. Holborn, *Refugees*, p. 518.
9. Dirks, pp. 234–35.
10. Reg Whitaker, *The Double Standard: The Secret History of Canadian Immigration* (Toronto, 1987), p. 218.
11. Lisa Gilad, *The Northern Route: An Ethnography of Refugee Experiences* (St John's, Nfld, 1990), p. 309.

Chileans

The Enriquez Family

Carlos Piña and Elizabeth McLuhan

Life changed irrevocably for the Enriquez family after the military coup of 11 September 1973. Belisario Enriquez was an English literature professor at the University of Chile. After the coup led by General Pinochet, pro-Allende friends and associates started disappearing, only to be found dead later. Belisario Enriquez, like many others, had been an active Allende supporter. The police went to the Enriquez home to look for him after the coup. By then Belisario had gone into hiding.

The family had good reason to believe that Belisario's life was in danger. Maria Angelica and her husband had both lost their jobs because of their political affiliations. She was working as an actress at the theatre at the University of Chile and had already been interrogated by the police. Maria Angelica and her children were questioned in their home during the night by the military and their house was ransacked. Their neighbour was picked up earlier by the police and never returned.

Knowing that if he was arrested, he would suffer a similar fate, Belisario (with fifty other Chileans) sought asylum in the Canadian embassy in Santiago. The Chileans refused to leave. The Chileans' occupation of the embassy continued. The days stretched into weeks and weeks into months. Finally, the Canadian government sent a special ambassador to review the Chileans' cases in their embassy. A special Canadian armed forces plane was sent to airlift the asylum seekers and their families to Canada.

The Enriquez family arrived in Canada on 11 January 1974. Maria Angelica and her husband had three children: Gabriela (the oldest), Fernan, and Claudio. Today, Claudio, an architecture student, lives at home. Fernan is married with a second child on the way. Gabriela, also married, has a four-year-old daughter named Valentina, and was also pregnant at the time of the interview. When they arrived in Canada, Gabriela was ten years old, Fernan was eight, and Claudio was six. The violence they experienced in the wake of the military coup continues to haunt them, most especially Maria Angelica and her eldest child, Gabriela, who remembers so much of what she witnessed as a young girl.

In Chile, they were a middle-class family with a very stable economic status–a status that was virtually shattered with the death of Allende and the subsequent reign of terror. The change in their lives was a dramatic one. Fleeing for their lives, they were in Chile one day and in Canada the next. Canada was a country about which they knew nothing. Following relocation to Toronto, Belisario Enriquez helped other Chilean refugees because he was one of the few who spoke English. He was certain

6. The Enriquez family–Maria Angelica with Gabriela, Claudio, Fernan, and Belisario in Santiago, Chile, c. 1970 (Photo: courtesy of the Enriquez family)

they would be returning to Chile and that their situation was only temporary.

Within less than two years of their arrival, Belisario was dead from leukemia. The task of keeping the family together and ensuring their financial support fell entirely to Maria Angelica, who knew no English. Maria Angelica held several jobs before she decided to go back to college and become a community worker. Now at the Centre for Spanish-Speaking Peoples, she helps other refugees and immigrants. Over the years, she has continued to be involved in the arts.

The children are now grown up. Fernan is a musician. Claudio is finishing his studies in architecture. Gabriela sells crafts from Chile. They have retained their mother tongue and all of them have been back to Chile several times. The Enriquez family lives in a co-op housing development in the heart of Toronto with about forty other families, most of whom are Chileans who arrived as refugees.

The Enriquez Family Speaks

Interviewed by Carlos Piña and Elizabeth McLuhan

Maria Angelica Nuñez Enriquez My name is Maria Angelica Nuñez Enriquez. I was born in Santiago, Chile. At the time of the coup, I was married with three children. I come from an artistic family. When I was fifteen or sixteen years old, I decided to study theatre at the University of Chile. I worked in theatre and television for many years.

I acted mostly in Chilean plays because of my face and very dark hair. I started working at the university in 1966 in one of the plays by the Nobel Prize poet, Pablo Neruda. We worked very closely with Neruda. It was very nice to know him not only as a poet but as a playwright.

On 11 September 1973, there was a military coup and the government of Salvador Allende was toppled. At that time, my husband was a professor of English literature at the University of Chile and the general secretary of the Faculty of Philosophy and Education, a very high position at the university. He was also a member of the Communist party in Chile. The Department of Philosophy and Education had sided with Salvador Allende.

On the day of the coup, the first thing the military did was to go to the university. My husband's office was searched by the military. Communist party members were accused of planning to assassinate someone. They said they found some arms, maps, and plans in his office. Those were all lies; he didn't even know how to use a gun. The police were looking for all of the people who were involved in politics at the university.

The police went to our previous house. Because we had moved and the university didn't have our new address, the police went to the old house to look for Belisario about a week after the coup. The people who were living in the house told them they didn't know anything about us, but when the military left, they communicated with us and told us what happened. We understood my husband's life was very much in danger. He was related to one of the leaders of a leftist movement in Chile. We think the police were looking for him also because he was related, and his last name became very dangerous. There weren't many people with the same last name. We had to use our second last name.

My husband didn't want to leave the country. By November or December, many people were leaving, trying to get into the embassies because their lives were in great danger. Finally, the police found our new house and they searched it. He was not living at home any more, and I told them I was separated. I believe many people said the same thing at that time. I told them I was living all by myself.

We had already talked to our kids and told them what had happened in the country. We also told them not to talk to the police and never to say anything, just to act like they don't know anything. The kids were ten, eight, and almost six, but they were very much involved with us in volunteer community work during the Allende administration. They knew a lot about what had happened in Chile.

Frank Teruggi, our American neighbour, was found killed in the street. We knew that my husband's life was very much in danger, too. If they did something like this to Frank, they would do something like this to him. My husband was still going to the university, but later people told him not to go because he was in so much danger. Then the university was closed.

I was working at the university's theatre. We were expelled from the theatre. We were told not to set foot in the theatre anymore. I lost my job. Many of my friends were taken, and some of the people at the theatre disappeared.

Meanwhile, my husband was living in different places, moving from one place to another place. And many times I didn't know his whereabouts, but other people told me he was okay and I should not be worried. I didn't talk to him for security reasons.

My husband had some friends living in France. These people were working at UNESCO and tried to communicate with us. They told us maybe it would be a good idea if he left for France, but the French embassy was surrounded by the military and besides, there were many people inside the embassy. He met one of the high commissioners of the French embassy, who told him that the French embassy didn't have more space, it was so crowded. He also had some communication with the Swedish ambassador and with one of the representatives of the Canadian embassy.

The man working for the French embassy communicated with the Canadian and told him to let people go inside the Canadian embassy. I know that the Canadian embassy didn't want to. I think they argued that Canada didn't sign some kind of agreement and that's why they didn't want the people to go inside, but they opened the door for one day to let the people go in.

My husband was then taken by this person from the French embassy to the Canadian embassy, which was located in the middle of downtown Santiago. Many people went into the embassy that day. We thought he was going to leave for France. I was informed that I was going to have to get some money for the tickets. At that time, I didn't have any money because we had both lost our jobs. I was trying to reach some friends to find out the best way to leave the country.

I believe that later there was some conversation with the embassy and the Canadian government. Finally, they decided to take the group to Canada. At that time they told us that we were going to Montreal. Inside the embassy, there were about 100 people. It was very crowded.

They lived there for a month. It was not very big and had only offices. One day I received information that Canada would allow the wives and children to come, too, and that we should get passports. My father knew some people and I got my passport very fast.

It was very uncertain. We didn't know what to do. I didn't know what was going to happen to my husband, and the situation in Chile was getting worse and worse. People were disappearing. People were killed. Some of our best friends were killed, and the situation was getting really uncertain. I didn't know what the future was for me.

The children felt terrible, their father was gone, and there was a curfew and you couldn't go outside. Besides, you didn't trust many people because you didn't know who people were. In our case, many of our friends were gone. You would talk to some people and overhear stories that something had happened with this one, something happened to that one, somebody was killed. You just live in fear. You don't know what is going to happen.

When I was informed that we were going to leave the country, I was happy and unhappy. I didn't want to leave my family, my father, mother, brother. I felt as though I wasn't deciding for myself. Somebody else was deciding for me what I should do, that I should leave the country. But I also wanted to be secure with my children and my family. Finally we left the country. That was on 10 January 1974. A military aircraft came from Canada, a big plane. We all left on the same plane.

We had to go inside the embassy. Some people were screaming at us and some people were saying goodbye. They took us on buses to the airport. We were only allowed to bring two pieces of luggage. In the end, we brought mostly toys that were important to the kids. It was very difficult. I didn't know what to take. I didn't know what was important in the house. I didn't know what was going to happen with the whole house, my car, the furniture, all the photos we had, ornaments. And they said we could only take two pieces of luggage–from our whole way of life!

When we were on the plane, they told us that we were not going to Montreal, we were going to Toronto. I knew very little about Canada at that time. I knew there were two languages–French and English. Because my husband spoke English, he thought that maybe Toronto would be the place for us. I also

7. The Enriquez family boarding the Canadian Forces plane that was to take them to Toronto, 1974 (Photo: courtesy of the Enriquez family)

knew it was very cold, but I never knew it was as cold as it was. It never crossed my mind.

January is summer in Chile, and I was dressed for summer. I put on another pair of socks. I thought maybe double socks would be good, and two sweaters would be good. What a surprise! When we arrived in Canada, it was terrible. Never in my life have I felt cold like that. Besides, I didn't have the right shoes because when I was leaving, I didn't think about any other kinds of shoes–boots. I had tried to get better winter clothing for my kids, but I was thinking about the Chilean winter, not the Canadian winter. We arrived on 11 January at six in the morning.

When we left Chile, we were escorted by the military and police. We couldn't say goodbye to our family. We left Chile via Mexico. The Mexican government didn't allow us to exit the plane in Mexico. They refuelled the plane with us inside, and only allowed us to open the door for the kids because it was hot inside–very, very hot.

Afterwards we flew to Toronto. When we arrived, they took

us all into a big room and made us wait for a medical exam. There were some doctors to see if we were all in good health. Then they took us to our hotel and gave us some food. They took us to this place called Ontario Welcome House. At that time it was very close to Harbourfront. We got some clothing and they gave us some other stuff, too.

We lived at the hotel for a while. The government was paying for the hotel. They said that we could stay at the hotel a maximum of two months. We stayed two months. There were some Chilean students living in Toronto who helped us, and some other Canadians who were very much involved with Chile and helped the whole group. They tried to place everybody. For us, it was difficult because we had three kids.

In the whole group, there were not many people who spoke English. I would say only two or three, and my husband was the only one who could speak English well. He was always needed to translate, to go to the doctor because someone got sick, and to take people different places. That's why we stayed in the hotel–because he was helping others move out of the hotel. That's why the people in charge told us not to worry–they knew he didn't have time to look for his own place and they needed him as an interpreter. We were left at the hotel and for us, it was something so different.

It was January; it was so cold. We didn't know the city and were always wondering about our family in Chile. We didn't have much communication with them. The newspaper didn't print much about what was going on in Chile. We felt very separated. These Canadian groups were very nice to us–there was a sense of solidarity, but when we walked in the street, we found the people cold. Even the way people lived was different from us. Immediately, we felt we were in a very different place from our home.

Finally, we moved to a flat on the west side of the city. We rented the second floor from a Portuguese family. The parents didn't speak English, but their kids spoke English.

You had to get used to a new kind of life, living in a flat, and sharing the house with other people who were very different from us. They played music that was not our music, and were very loud. They cooked different foods and the smells were completely different.

We collected some furniture, plates, things that we needed for the house. My husband was always thinking that we were going to leave soon, that the military was not going to last very long, and that we were going to return to Chile in two months, three months, no more than six months. You always have that in mind, but I said that I couldn't live with that. I have to build my nest for the security of the kids. We had to do something.

There was a school nearby, and we sent the kids to school. We went to meetings for the Chileans. We thought the government was going to fall and didn't think we would be here permanently. They were giving English language classes to the men. They didn't want to give classes to women, especially to women married with kids. We had to fight to get people to give us the opportunity to have ESL classes.

I thought it was very important to learn English. In the Portuguese family, the lady didn't speak English, the father spoke only broken English, and the kids spoke only English. I could understand when the lady spoke to the kids in Portuguese because Portuguese is very similar to Spanish. She told them not to speak to her in English because she couldn't understand. I could picture myself with the same problem. I thought, if I don't understand this language, this is what is going to happen to me. We were a very close family and I didn't want to see myself in this situation. This poor woman was screaming, "I don't understand you." That's why we met with other women and we made some noise, and finally the government gave us the opportunity to go to the ESL classes.

We all came as refugees. When we were all in the embassy in Chile, we were interviewed by Canadian immigration. They started the papers in Santiago and after a while, many people received their landed immigrant papers. I believe there were two who never received their landed immigrant papers. One was a person who had to leave for Spain, and the other was my husband. He never received his papers as a landed immigrant. One day I went to immigration to ask for an extension of our minister's permit. We all had minister's permits to stay in the country. I saw my husband's file. His file had a lot of things written on it–TOP SECRET–maybe because he was a member of the Communist party. I don't know the reason. Until the day he died here in Canada, he never received the landed immigrant papers. I only received the papers two years after his death.

Belisario was healthy when he came to this country, but he got leukaemia in 1975, after a year in Canada. He had had a very bad cold and went to the hospital, where they found he had leukaemia. In January 1976, he passed away at Mount Sinai Hospital. He lived with acute leukaemia for two months.

We were left without him in a new country, almost two years after we arrived. We were not allowed to go back to Chile: his name was on a list of those forbidden to return.

I made my home in Toronto while he was alive, but when he passed away, I had many options to go to different countries. I had many friends and some thought we should go elsewhere. I didn't want to move because I didn't want to take the kids again to another country, to pack up and leave everything behind. I was feeling so lonely here, no family, no relatives.

The Chileans here were not my friends from my earlier life; we only met on the plane or here. It's not like the friendships you build in your own country. And they were so different from us. In many ways by imposition, you had to be friends to people, not because you decided. They were very nice people, but at that time, it was difficult.

No family, no money. I thought maybe I should move to France, and I flew to France with my daughter. I had been in France before, but always as a tourist. When I went to France, again it was beautiful, always lots of cultural activities. But again, it was a different language, and the Medicare was not so secure.

I decided to come back to Canada. We stayed in France for four weeks, and I came back to Canada again. When the plane was landing, I saw the CN tower and I said, "Oh, I'm coming home." It was strange; it was the first time I thought of Canada as my home. That's why I decided to live in Canada.

When my husband was dying, I didn't know about social services like welfare. Nobody told me. It was not publicized. I was working at Sears. My husband was working as a cleaner at the University of Toronto and was taking courses at OISE. I had to leave Sears when my husband died.

After that, it became very difficult for me to keep the house and look after the kids. It was a very big shock to me to be left so far away from my own country with no family to help. I had to be so strong for my kids. It was really hard.

I started a part-time job at the Art Gallery of Ontario as a salesperson and also handled art rentals. I was also working at another small gallery, the Inuit Gallery of Eskimo Art, and I liked it. I was trying to get into the arts by doing some kind of poetry reading or teaching Chilean dancing. I was trying to work at something related to my previous profession. And that's the way my year passed—working in this gallery and working with the solidarity for Chile, too.

I decided to go to George Brown College and took a course in community work. I graduated in that course and I started to work in community service.

I am presently working at the Centre for Spanish-Speaking Peoples, helping refugees or new immigrants to resettle here. Mostly, I give them information. Some come without knowing much about Canada, or the weather, or the way of life here. For us, Canada is a very different society.

Imagine that you're coming from a different country and the next day you are in a big city with subways, buses, and clothing so different from what you are used to. The shops are so big and people don't really understand what other people are talking about. You buy so many tokens for a dollar, and you pay the token, and you take the transfer. Newcomers say, "What are you talking about? Transfers? Tokens? Subways?" I say people need to talk to someone, one by one, rather than in a big group of people; to go to a centre where things can be explained to them.

That's mostly what I am doing. I just give information, and try to explain how they can get a job and how they can go to school. All of that was really difficult for me and for many people when we first came to this country.

Maybe because of the weather here, people seem to be very private. Not like us Chileans, we are a more open society. In Chile, because of the weather, we spend more time outside, and we know our neighbours, we know the people. But in this country, people tend to be more private. You don't know much about other people. It can be difficult to make friends.

People tend to forget they were once immigrants here. They are maybe second-generation people, and their parents were hard-working when they came to this country. And because they have been here longer than we have, they think they own the land. I feel that discrimination sometimes, but I think it is based on ignorance.

I don't think I feel Canadian. No, I feel part of the country, part of this society, but it's difficult to feel really Canadian. I feel like a part of the country; I like the country. At the beginning, it was really difficult for me to get used to the society of the country, but by now, I have very good friends. My children are growing. I have grandchildren. I'm part of the country, but it's very strange–inside I always know I am Chilean. I feel Chilean.

I feel very proud of this country, especially when I am watching the news and Canada does something good, like when the Blue Jays won in baseball. I feel good. I feel very happy to be living in this country.

I have good memories about Chile. I think the people of Chile are very warm. I sometimes miss things about Chile, like the people, the smell, but I am used to Canada. I feel Canada is well organized; everything works. I hate bureaucracy, and in Chile, everything was so difficult, so bureaucratic.

I have not lived in Chile for so long, about eighteen years. I was there in 1985 for a few weeks. Sometimes I think that if I went back to Chile and lived there, what would I do? All my friends are gone. Maybe I'm afraid to go back and start to make friends all over again. I don't know what happened to the ones that I had. Many of them died and many of them left Chile, too. And we have probably changed so much because we have lived in different places.

When I was in Chile in 1985, I felt different. Because I left the country, many thought that I had not suffered. Because they stayed, they suffered a lot during all these years of the dictatorship. I tried to explain that I was not going to compare my suffering to theirs because it was completely different. I understand that the people who stayed in Chile suffered dictatorship every day and every night and I have great sympathy for that. But to be outside of the country was very painful, too, in another way. It is difficult to make any kind of comparison.

People in Chile are happy to see you, but they remind you that you weren't there with them when everything was going on in Chile. I am not afraid to go back because of that, it's only that we have been living apart for so long. Our lives are so separate now, I can't see myself again in Chile. I don't know if I fit in anymore. Maybe that's why I am afraid to go back. I don't want to go there by myself and have the same thing happen to my grandchildren as when we came to Canada: the children were separated from their grandparents and uncles.

Once we were a very close family in Chile. The kids loved their grandparents and uncles. I believe the kids really missed their family. One of my sons developed some kind of asthma. I'm sure the kids had a lot of problems to cope with a new country. In Canada, it was very difficult for the kids to make friends with the neighbours, even when we lived in the same house with the Portuguese family.

When we were living in that flat, I heard that some Chileans were living in Etobicoke, and I decided to move there. The kids made friends with other Chileans, playing soccer and hockey. They were happier.

The Chilean families were much closer to me, which helped me to cope. They would take us out, sometimes in the car. We started to feel warmer towards the country–between Chileans–but not integrated with Canadians.

I imagine my future is here; tomorrow, I don't know what is going to happen. In three or four or ten years, I don't know, but I am living in Canada today. I'm happy to be living in Canada.

My children feel very much Canadian, Chilean-Canadian also. All of them speak Spanish, all of them are in some way connected to Latin America or Chile.

Gabriela, my older daughter, is married to a Chilean. She met Chileans when she was allowed to go back to Chile. She has been

8. The Enriquez family in the courtyard of their co-op homes, from left: Claudio, Maria Angelica, Gabriela, and Fernan, 1993 (Photo: Vincenzo Pietropaolo)

in Chile three times. She took her daughter twice, and she is only four years old. She has a very strong relationship with Chile. She sells Chilean and Latin American crafts to Canadians.

One of my sons is a musician, and he plays Latin American music. He has also been to Latin America and Chile a few times. He is married to a French woman. The French are very close to us as a society, as a way of living. My other son is the only one who is single. He travelled for seven months in Latin America, Central America, and Chile. They all speak Spanish well, and I believe they are very much attached to Chile.

My grandchildren are Canadian. My granddaughter understands Spanish; my grandson has three languages: Spanish, English, and French. I think we feel very much Canadian, but in our home, there are so many things that are Latin American. Maybe we feel more Latin American now; Chilean, yes, but part of all of Latin America. This is important because many times it was as though we were very isolated in Chile.

The people my children bring home are Latin American, Chilean, or many others. And they are Canadian. Many cultures come together in this country.

Because I was forced to leave my country, I always have in the back of my mind that I moved by necessity to this country. In order to survive, I settled here. This is always in my mind. I know that I am not here originally by choice and that is difficult.

But now that I have worked in this country, paid my taxes, I do everything that other people do here, now I feel I am a part of the country. But, at the same time, I always feel that I am an outsider because of the language, because of the way I live.

I think the politics are the same here as in Chile, the same as everywhere else. The average person doesn't understand much.

In Chile, people are more involved in politics or in any kind of movement that is happening. But maybe I'm talking about twenty years ago; it's difficult to say with eighteen years in between. I remember that we used to be very much involved with everything. We would do volunteer work or participate in the campaign. Whatever we were doing, there was much participation in the country. For example, in the arts we knew inside out about our artists, the theatre, television, about what happened with the Chilean people.

Maybe because Canada is so big, sometimes people don't really know what happens here. They take so many things for granted. They don't really value the people. Maybe they miss a little nationalism, like we have in Chile. That's something that I don't always quite understand about Canada.

I was talking to a friend. I said, "How can you hang a Canadian flag as a curtain in the window? We would never do something like this in Chile." And the person said, "It's only a flag." I said, "It's only a flag, but that flag reflects the country. It's the country's symbol," and they said, "Who cares? It's nothing; it's a piece of material." I don't think in Chile we would use the Chilean flag as a curtain. We would never do something like that.

As a refugee, it's so strange. One day you are in your country, and the next day you are in a new country where it is cold. I'm from the middle class, but in Chile, we would never waste anything. For example, you go to buy drinks or wine, you take your bottles and you give them to the person at the counter and they give you the wine. We didn't waste so much stuff. It is amazing what they waste in this country. Boxes for this, boxes for that, plastics; so much waste.

That's what I felt when I came to this country. I was trying to keep so much stuff in my house: so much garbage and new stuff. No one here repairs things: if your socks need darning, you put them in the garbage. In Latin America, you fix your socks. That was something I couldn't understand when I came. People couldn't understand poverty, and why we try so hard to fight against it. Many countries in Latin America are very poor. They are very rich in material resources, but there were many poor people. My husband, myself, many of my friends, and many others worked for a governnment that would give all children food, milk, education, health, so people would have the opportunity to see a doctor or a dentist, to eat, to have a proper house.

Sometimes you have to nationalize some of the national resources. In Chile, for example, the land belonged to very few families. Many people didn't have land for planting or for their own food. The resources were in the hands of very few people. Many people were left on the sidelines. We had to leave the country because the military took power, and because the big multinationals didn't like losing everything that they'd had in Chile. There is so much difference between poor people and those with money. The resources were not well distributed.

Today we are amazed to see this in Somalia, to see so much poverty over there. Nobody knew for so many years. But in Latin American countries, people have been suffering for a long time. The Native community also has been fighting for years to survive in Central and South America. Because we were so much involved in this kind of politics, we had to leave the country.

We have kept in touch with relatives by letters, and they occasionally phone. My sister, who was living in Europe, invited my parents and she paid for the tickets. They came through Canada, and the kids had the opportunity to see their grandparents. Aside from that, we always communicated by letters. My sister also once came from Europe to see us.

We moved to this townhouse in 1981 or 1980. A group of Chileans living in Etobicoke started this co-op. I was so happy because one of them said to me, "You will never have problems here; you are going to have your own house with the kids, don't worry about that." When you are living by yourself in an apartment with kids, it's tough. People don't want to rent an apartment to you. They say, "You are woman; who is going to support you?" I had that experience many times.

I had so much hope in this co-op where everybody was going to live. I remember so many meetings, and going to the government to raise money to build the house. I was a member of the board of directors of the co-op that built the houses. It was a big change when we moved to these co-op houses.

Most of the families are from Chile, but not all of them. We can see our children growing up in the co-op, living in the co-op, marrying in the co-op. Two of mine are married. One is my neighbour and the other lives across the garden. I have two and a half grandchildren because one is coming in January—my son's.

Gabriela Enriquez I was just ten or eleven years old when I left Chile. We left Chile on the 11 January 1974. I remember the day. I remember how everybody was so tense, and for the first time, I heard bombs, people running, people screaming. I could hear the military going by. I could see there was something totally wrong in my neighbourhood, where I used to feel very secure. My parents kept saying, "Do not open the door for anybody. Do not look out the window at night. Do not get up if anybody comes—just stay in your bed. Do not go anywhere."

Most of my friends supported the Allende government, even my teacher. The most secure place was school because a teacher would always look after you, but one day when we arrived at school, the military came. They came to our classroom. They started taking all the children out of the classroom and putting them against the wall. The first classroom, of course, was the kindergarten; I could see that they were coming out first. I sensed that something was wrong. The kids in the classroom—we were only ten years old—were all getting very scared.

The military were looking for the teachers. That day, they took our principal to jail because she used to have very good connections with Allende.

I think my teacher was socialist or something like that and they said they were going to take her, but they didn't in the end. I don't know what happened. They came into our classroom. They told us all to sit down at our desks. There were two military men at the door and one inside the classroom and they started looking for things. They didn't find anything and they left. But we knew that our teacher kept a picture of Allende in one of her books. The military people didn't see it, so when they left, one of

9. Maria Angelica Nuñez Enriquez, her daughter Gabriela, and peeking out from between them, her grandchildren, Valentina and Xavier, Toronto, 1993 (Photo: Vincenzo Pietropaolo)

the students started looking and found the picture and we took it and ripped it up.

It's like a big block of memories, that day. The day of the coup, we were almost the first ones to hear that Allende was killed. My father knew lots of people and he was worried about them, so he started looking for our friends and trying to make sure that they were safe.

One day, around eight o'clock at night, a big tank came down our street. The military started searching house by house. They were looking for somebody. They came to our house and started asking my mother where my father was and my mother said, "I don't know." The military man pretended to be very polite, but he had a mean face and a very sarcastic way of talking to my mother. But my mother was very quiet, very gentle, and she kept saying, "I don't know." He kept saying, "It's almost eight o'clock, it's almost curfew time. Where's your husband?" My mother kept saying, "I don't know, he should be coming any minute." So they came in and said they were going to search the house. The only thing my mother kept saying to me was, "Don't leave your brothers alone; don't leave your brothers alone."

They took us into our bedroom and started throwing everything on the floor. Our father was so strict about our keeping everything nice and tidy. They threw everything on the floor and made a big mess, even the laundry bag in the bathroom they turned upside down. I got really mad and said, "Look, please clean it up." The soldier just laughed. They took me into one bedroom, they took Fernan into another bedroom, and they took Claudio into another room. At that moment I thought, "Forget it." They just keep asking me all these questions about where my father was. So I went to find my brothers. The soldiers kept on asking them where my father was, if he was hiding inside the house, if there were guns inside the house. I kept saying there were no guns. We had a dog, a boxer, in the house, and the soldiers said for us to keep him in the garage or else they were going to shoot him. The dog was going wild. The dog was very protective.

Then the soldiers left, but they were very mad. They had turned the whole house upside down. It was an intrusion, coming into our house. They did not come to talk to my father, they came to take him away. I was worried that they would do something to my mother because they took her outside in the yard and it was so dark that I couldn't see a thing. She was gone for a long time, it seemed. When I saw my mother coming back inside, she was still okay. She still had her clothes on and nothing had happened to her. Then they went to the next house and they took our neighbour, Frank Teruggi, an American who was later found shot. I kept looking outside to see if my father was coming. I didn't know if my mother knew where he was or not. He didn't come home, and my mother said he was somewhere, but she never told us where he was. I never knew until we left the country. He was hiding and my mother kept saying, "He's okay. We'll see him one day." And then a month went by and my mother kept saying, "Your father is hiding. Don't worry."

One morning when I arrived at school, my teacher said that she was sorry my father was killed yesterday. I kept saying, "No." "But the dead man has the same last name," she said. I said, "I know, but my father is not dead." I was very worried and when I got home, I asked my mother. She kept saying, "No. It must be another person." Then we went to my grandparents' house. My grandmother was crying. The military had come looking for my father. They slapped my grandmother, who was an old woman. My poor grandfather, who was outside, was hysterical. These two people were so gentle. They had raised seven children, and were always so nice to us and never hurt anybody. They looked afraid and were trying not to transmit it to me, especially because I was a kid, but I could see it in their faces. The military totally abused them–they were mean and terrible.

My mother said we might go to France. They were trying to get my father to take refuge in the French embassy. I remember we were learning a little bit of French, so that when we got there, we would know something. We were not allowed to tell anybody about our plans. I didn't want to leave. I kept pleading with my mother. I didn't see my father. I kept telling her that I wanted to stay with my grandparents. I didn't want to leave Chile. I had my friends there; I had my family there. But even though everything was so dark and terrible, it seemed just as terrible to go to another place where we didn't have anything.

My mother kept saying to us that we couldn't take everything that belonged to us because we were going in an airplane. We could only take our dolls and some clothing. We could not take our dog, which we loved very much. When you're a kid, you worry about your house, you worry about your grandparents, your dog, and here I was leaving everything behind.

I remember that day we left was very sunny. It was a very hot day. We had only one suitcase that we could take with us. I had my doll in a little box with doll clothes. That's all we took. We weren't allowed to take anything else but a knapsack. We just had clothing because we had to leave the house without letting people know that we were going away. The rest of our belongings were left behind. Later, soldiers searched the house and robbed us of everything. In other words, we lost everything in the house.

We went to our grandparents' house and had a farewell dinner. I kept telling my mother it was late because we had to be at the embassy by three o'clock. It must have been two o'clock. I was very nervous because I wanted to see my father. The only time I had seen my father since he went into hiding was when we used to go into a little mall and we would look up to a building where the embassy was. Once in a while, my mother would tell us that we were going there. We would stand there for a few minutes, and wait for my father to appear in the window and wave to us, but we had to be very careful not to respond in a way that someone would see us. After he went into hiding, I never saw him until we went to the embassy. It must have been at least three months. There were snipers pointing towards the embassy windows, but that was the only chance we got to see my father, through a window high above us.

My grandmother told us that we had to take our possessions, so she put all our teddy bears and stuffed animals in a bag. When we got to the embassy, there were military men with machine-guns. We had to walk by them. It was not really such a long walk, but it felt like it.

When we got into a bus, all these people were screaming at us saying, "Communists! Get out of our country!" The military were everywhere. My grandmother and grandfather were waving at us, looking at us, with the biggest tears in their eyes as though we would never see them again.

When we got to the airport, we went through customs and the soldier was very, very rude. He kept saying, "Come over here, come over here," to the photographer and the media. "I want to show you this, I want to show you all the things these people are taking from this country." So he opened the big suitcase and all he found, to his surprise, were stuffed animals. Then we waited and waited, but my father didn't come. I could hear people saying that something must have happened. I started to cry. I thought we would have to leave without my father. Finally, my father arrived.

We left the country, not in a regular airplane, but in a military one. As soon as the plane took off, the pilot said, "You should look down because this is the last time you will see Chile for quite a long time." I remember that I wasn't sitting with my parents. Our family was scattered throughout the airplane. It seemed everybody started to cry. When we got to Mexico, it was very hot and we could not leave the airplane. And when we arrived in Canada, it was very cold–freezing cold. We had to go through customs and a medical exam at the airport. Then they took us to a place where they had cookies and drinks for us. It was the first time I saw Coca-Cola in cans. They gave us warm clothes and took us to the hotel. At the hotel, we were living in one little room with a little kitchen. It was the first time I saw colour TV. Those are the things I remember.

And then we were moved from one hotel to another. Then we rented two rooms on the second floor of a house. But in Chile, we had a house, we had a bed, we had our clothes, we had everything. Here we were almost begging. My father was a professional in Chile. But in Canada he could make a living only if he was willing to do something different. Here, we were renting a house from a Portuguese family. But my father, when we came here, always tried to make life special for us, so we have a very beautiful memory of my father in Canada. He took us everywhere, he took us to the park, we walked down Yonge Street, he took us for walks, and whenever he had a little bit of money, he would take us somewhere special.

We started going to school. My father kept saying to us, "This is only going to be for three, four, or five months." My father spoke English very well. He was always teaching us the language. I think I still have a tape of him trying to teach me English.

I didn't want to learn the language. For me, English was no use. I was going back to Chile. I was going back to how everything was before. I was going back to my house. I was going to play in my backyard with my dog. I was going to go back to school. Learning English was not important, even though the teacher tried to be nice and teach me the language. He kept saying one thing and I would say another. I thoroughly refused the language because it didn't make sense to learn it. I wasn't going to stay here.

And then my father got sick and died. That was, I think, the worst nightmare that I ever had. After that, things changed and, for me, there was no life anymore because I lost someone that I loved so much. We were there all by ourselves in a country we didn't even know, a country we didn't even want to be in, a country that didn't want us because we weren't welcomed at that time.

We had nothing. We were sleeping on the floor. When we first moved into the house, I would wake up at night and feel something crawling on my face. I knew right away it was a cockroach. For me, it was a total change. As years go by, you try to analyse the whole thing because you're trying to get your life back together. We didn't want to be here. We were forced to be here. My father was forced to come here. If we had had a choice, maybe he would have been here in Canada by himself and we would have stayed in Chile by ourselves, which wasn't very practical because my mother would have been on her own with three children. Her friends were being taken. They were doing all sorts of horrible things at that time. People didn't have morals in that country. So we came here and we had to live here.

I didn't want to be here, but I made Canadian friends at school. My first Canadian friend was a girl named Sharon. Even though I was the only one who didn't speak any English, my Canadian friends kept talking to me. She was very nice. She protected me. Then we moved to Etobicoke where we were so discriminated against that it was a real down part of our lives. The Spanish people were on one side and Canadians were on the other. A whole gang of Canadian youths were harassing Chileans, especially the children. It was like the gangs in movies–it was that bad. The police didn't seem to care. There was a big fight one day right in the middle of the park. I'm glad nobody got killed. There were people stabbing each other with pens. That's how I got the feeling that I wasn't part of the system, because of the discrimination and the harassment. You could feel it.

We would walk down to the Dominion to buy something. We would get stopped, we'd get kicked, and since I was the oldest one, I was always trying to protect my brothers, so I always got the punches and kicks. I always told my brothers to run. It was so painful to see my brothers get hit. I went right in and defended them and I told them to run home. I was kicked and punched. The best change was moving downtown to the co-op. It was the best thing that ever happened to us because it gave us more independence. My mother felt we would be safer living beside other people from other cultures, but we were living in an apartment full of cockroaches. I'd never seen cockroaches in my life.

At school, they put me in the lowest level because I didn't

speak any English and I had an accent. When I was in grade eight, my teacher put me into the lowest level. He never talked to me, he never came to me, he never said anything to me to help me learn more English. It seemed that they never cared whether I wanted to learn the language; I had to learn it all by myself, and I had to force myself because when my father died there was nobody else to teach me.

Actually, it didn't take me that long to learn. My first teacher that I had in grade five was a wonderful teacher, and the terrible thing is that I knew what he was saying, but I didn't want to learn. So he kept talking to me and I kept saying I don't want to learn the language. He kept showing me this card saying, "This is a turkey, and this is a chicken. What is this?" He kept showing me the turkey card and I would say, "Chicken." I kept playing this game with him. He got me to play chess at school. Whenever he spoke, I understood everything–that was the worst thing. But nobody pushed me to speak English except my first teacher.

When we moved to Old Mill, there was a very large community of people who spoke Spanish and it was not that hard for me to think about learning the English language. But in school, the teacher was always putting me down. When you come to this country as a refugee, you are already very demoralized. You need someone to help you get started. I had lost my father and had just moved into a new neighbourhood and was going to a different school. The school was putting me down and I was already feeling down, so I just didn't want to do anything. I wouldn't do anything so I could better myself. My mother was the only one who pushed us, saying that we had to learn the language, we had to go to school. I kept saying, "Why? I am going to go back to Chile. Why do I have to do this?" I lived all the time thinking that one day I was going to go back to Chile because some of my best memories were there.

Then my grandfather died and everything became more complicated. I wanted to be with my grandparents, I wanted to be beside them. I wanted to be beside my father and my father wasn't there, and now my grandfather wasn't there anymore either. My other grandfather had died too, so everybody close to me was dying. Then it seemed that I became a person with no country, in a way. Here I was in Canada and I didn't feel Canadian, but I wasn't a Chilean either. I didn't know what I was, where I should be, what I should be learning, or how I should be feeling. My father had just passed away. I was all by myself with my mother and my brothers.

I always think it's important at that age that everything should be in place. My mother was working in a factory and she had never worked in a factory before. She had had a wonderful profession in Chile. She was an actress. She had her career just starting for her and now she was here working in a factory. I always had to protect my brothers and take care of them. I was the one in charge of the house, making sure that the house was clean, that my brothers were eating, that nothing happened to them when they went to school. When they went to play outside, I had to protect them to make sure that nothing happened to them. There were gangs of people out there, and there were fights, so I became more like a protector of my brothers and the family. Things became better when we got older and moved downtown.

I started realizing that people were dying and there was nothing I could do. And then I started feeling like a person with nothing. My mother kept saying, "What's wrong with you? Why do you feel that way?" But I didn't know.

I think Chile is a beautiful country. It has a different way of living. It is a very family-oriented kind of country, and you always feel so secure, you always have friends and family coming over. Canada is very cold in a way, not very family-oriented. Here, once you turn eighteen, that's it. You leave home and make your own living. In Chile, it seems you are always part of the family. I feel I am a person living in Canada and I'm happy with that. I tell my husband and my mother that I would never go back to Chile to live again because I don't want to see my kids in a country where you can be so insecure that anything could happen to them or to us. I'm scared of going through the same process again. It could happen again and it could even happen here in Canada. I hope it never happens here in Canada. It did happen in Chile. You don't like the government, so you kill the people who support it–that's it. I just don't want to go through that again. I can never feel secure going back to Chile. I would love to go there and have a good time and see my friends and talk with them, but I couldn't live there again.

The first time I went back to Chile, I cried nearly all the way. I was twenty-one years old. When I got to Chile, it was hot, and the airport had changed. I wanted to be in Chile. It was my identity. My grandmother was going to be there, my grandfather wasn't. Then I got off the airplane and I went through customs. They took my Chilean passport away, and I knew something was wrong. At first, they said my name wasn't Enriquez, that I was a male. According to their computer, I was a man. I said their computer was wrong. The official kept saying, "You have one brother." And I said, "No, I have two brothers." He kept saying the only brother, according to the computer, is Claudio Enriquez. He took me to an office and then I met the person in charge of the airport. He was very mean, very strict, and he had a big picture behind his chair. He told me to sit down and said I was not allowed in the country because when I left, I left as a refugee. At that time, they had a big list of all the people who couldn't come back. I kept saying, "No, I went to the embassy; they gave me a passport. I talked to the person in charge at the consulate two days before I left. I wasn't on the list." I was not a threat to the country because when I left, I was only a kid. He said, "You are twenty-one years old, plus thirteen days. If you were younger than twenty-one, we could have let you into the country because children who left the country and return before they are twenty-one are allowed into Chile." He kept saying, "No, you can't come in." He left me there. I was crying my head off. I said, "My grandmother is outside. Why don't you tell her that this is going on and maybe they can do something." He went out to look for my grandmother. My grandmother said, "I'm looking for my granddaughter. Her name is Gabriela Enriquez. Is she inside the airport?" He kept saying that there was nobody inside, but other people who worked there told her, "She's in the back. She's being held. She's arrested in the back of the airport."

At that time, there was a friend of mine who used to live here in Canada, who was working in radio and had a press pass. She got in and did a whole interview of me inside the airport that day. When we left the country, we were blacklisted. My mother wasn't on the list and Fernan wasn't either, but I was and Claudio was.

I was detained for at least seven hours. I was on the radio because my friend had a tape recorder and she taped me. When the official left the room, my friend asked me what happened. So I talked because I was totally desperate. That's how some of my best friends found out I was in Chile.

Then they said that I had to go to Mandosa for the weekend to get a special permit so I could enter Chile. It was Saturday and everything was closed until Monday, so I wouldn't be back in Chile until Tuesday. My grandmother said, "Okay, I will go with you." They kept saying that I had to pay for my ticket. I said, "No, you pay me for my ticket. I am not going anywhere." Five minutes before I had to board the plane, the chief of security came in, hugged me, kissed me, and said, "Welcome to the country. I'm so sorry." Two ministers had signed a waiver saying that I could stay in the country. I didn't even have to go through customs. I didn't have to be checked.

I was going to stay in Chile for three months, but for the first week, I couldn't go out because I didn't have my passport. I wasn't able to hold on to my passport. I couldn't go out on the street in case somebody asked me for my documents. They took my passport and all my documents. In Chile, you are always asked for your documents and your ID. You can't go out unless you have your ID.

I think I needed that experience because I suddenly realized that Chile had not changed. It was still the same, but I was happy to be there. Nothing mattered anymore, I was just so happy to be there. I really wanted to be there. I wanted to be back in Chile, to be in Santiago, seeing my friends and family. I was really, really happy.

When I came back to Canada, my goal was to return to Chile and study there. That's what I really wanted to do. That was my goal; I wanted to go back and study. But I never went back to Chile because when you go back to Chile, you need to have money. You need to have someone to stay with. You have to be responsible for all the things you are going to be doing there. You have your family there, but they can't take care of you because they have their own lives. They have their own things to do; they have their own jobs. They can't have somebody else there. To go back to Chile would mean that I would need a place to stay. I would need money to be there. I needed to go back to school. But here in Canada, I was living with a single mother, with two other children. My mother was going back to school trying to get her life back together again. I am not blaming her. I am saying that because of circumstances at the time, I couldn't ask something of my mother that she didn't have. I've never asked anything of her that it wasn't possible for us to have. My mother was a single person. She was thinking of the three of us. She came to this country, she lost her husband, she lost her house, she lost her profession, she lost her family. She lost everything. She did everything that she could as a mother. She protected us, she made sure we were not doing drugs, that we were studying and going to school. We had many problems, but we were good, respectable people.

I didn't have the money to go back to Chile to study. I found out how much university would cost me there. There were some grants I could have applied for, but I still needed money to live there, and that was not possible. I began to realize that Chile existed, but I couldn't go back there anymore.

I imagine my future here in Canada. I want to keep my heritage. Other people who live in Canada also have different backgrounds–England, France, Russia, Italy, Portugal. It's good to keep that identity. You make a country grow and that's what makes Canada so interesting. There are so many different cultures. They can become one part of the system you know.

It was very difficult for me when I was young because then I did not have to speak the language, I had so many Spanish friends. Even now, if I don't go to work, I don't have to speak English. If I talk to someone on the phone, or if I talk to some of my best friends, then I speak to them in English, but I talk with the people of this community in Spanish. I talk to my daughter or my husband in Spanish. I have no problem with the two languages.

I'm not worried about my daughter's identity. She already has her identity. I didn't have an identity because I was taken from one place and put in another where I didn't feel I belonged. I lost everything I had once as a child. I don't want to go back to Chile because I'm scared that one day if I moved back, someone who doesn't like the system would change it and people would get caught in the middle. I don't want to go through that again. Actually, I could never go through what my mother went through. I think she did a wonderful job. I wish she would marry again. She would have another life. She always put family first before anything else in her life.

When I go back to Chile, I feel like I've been there all my life. I can speak the language, I have no accent. I feel really good about myself. Here in Canada, I speak with an accent. I think when I talk in Spanish and when I talk in English, it's like having two people inside of me. There are some feelings I have that I can't express in Spanish because they have no meaning or sense to them. But there are feelings I can only express in English because they mean something to me. I can use the two languages for different things. It feels good to be able to be part of two different systems. You are not stuck with one system. So I have two countries I can feel good about. I can go back to Chile. I can live in Canada. And I can feel good in going to either of the two countries. I can have an escape. If something happens here, I can always say, "Oh, well, I'm going back to Chile for a couple of months." If I don't like it there, I can always come back to Canada. Canada for me is a more secure place. I know nothing can happen to me and my family here.

Fernan Enriquez I was nine when we left Santiago. I remember we went from my house to the Canadian embassy in Santiago and there was heavy security on the part of the Chilean government around the Canadian embassy. We had to cross barricades to go into the building. From the embassy, we all left in a special bus for the airport. We knew we were going on a trip—we children actually knew what was going on. We knew we were going away, but we thought it was temporary. We left Santiago on a Canadian air force plane. It was the first time we had ever been on a plane.

My earliest memories of Toronto were of winter and snow. We came from a very hot climate right into mid-January. We arrived in Toronto and were taken to the Waldorf Astoria Hotel on Charles Street before it was renovated. We knew we were in a different place. There was the colour TV, and the shows were in a different language. There were elevators, escalators.

I think the government gave my family some money, and we were able to find a small flat in the Portuguese area here in Toronto. As soon as we found an apartment, we entered school, as I remember doing some Valentine's Day activities. As children, we picked up English pretty fast. Maybe within three months, we were communicating.

The school had a very large number of Portuguese immigrants, and there was a special class for people who did not know English. We ended up going with other kids who were trying to learn the language. I felt different from the other kids, speaking a different language. At that time, whenever someone on the street looked Spanish, I would run up to talk to them.

We moved to Etobicoke where I went to a school called Park Lawn, and then for my high school to a school called Richview

10. Fernan Enriquez busking in the Toronto subway with his associate, Franklin Herrera, 1993 (Photo: Vincenzo Pietropaolo)

Collegiate Institute. I always felt very different from the people there.

I got interested in music when I was about fifteen. I was working in a café that was playing Greek and Latin American music and ever since then, I've been playing the guitar and other South American folk instruments.

I started playing with a group of friends here in Toronto. Being of the same nationality, we would get together and play music. The one who did not know how to play the guitar or flute would begin by playing the drum–percussion. We would meet quite often–how do you call it–jamming. If you played with us long enough, in the end you would play twenty different instruments. I play guitar, charango (a ten-string instrument), the drum, pan flute, a kena (which is like a whistle), and tarkas (which are whistles that come in different sizes).

Each of us, we would play a little bit of everything. We

wouldn't be virtuosos on these instruments, but we would know maybe seven, eight, or ten notes and we could make a lot of songs out of that. We were doing some shows on the weekend, and organizing small concerts every once in a while. Canadian people really like our music. I always felt good playing music.

When I was seventeen or eighteen, I travelled to Mexico and eventually to Chile. The problem is that when you're in Canada, you're always feeling that you should be in Chile. Something pulls you there. But when you're there, you find out that there are a lot of things about Canada that pull you back.

When I went back for the first time, it was about eight years that I had been away from Chile. I felt very good there. I stayed about two weeks, and I fitted in very easily even though I hadn't been there for eight years. There was always the option in the back of my mind of eventually moving back, but the problem is that Chile is very unstable; I think Canada is much more stable.

I think of the state of mind of people at the time of my visit in Chile. They were really living in two worlds. They had one face that was a very happy face, but people were very careful of what they would say. How much they would talk depended on how well they knew you. Of course, they were not willing to be compromised in anything. At the same time, they would have that other face. If they had very strong opinions for or against the dictatorship, they would hide it. I think they were hiding a lot of themselves. So what you would see was a lot of fake people walking around, not because they wanted to be fake, just because they wanted to protect themselves and their families. I haven't taken a trip to Chile since the dictatorship fell. I haven't had a chance to see what it's like, but I've heard it's better and people are more relaxed.

My wife is from France and she has her family over there. She came to Canada as a nanny. It was like slavery. The nannies had no rights. They would go to a house to work as a nanny, and end up as a full-time, twenty-four-hour maid. If they didn't like it, they could just go back to France. That was the option they were given. It wasn't a very good experience. I met her at the St Lawrence Market here in Toronto.

Now that I am married and a father, I play music not only to enjoy myself but also to make a living. I play in the TTC subway stations. I think there are sixty-five subway stations. There are about thirty spots for musicians. They set times for us so we can have priority over other musicians on one spot.

Sometimes I play with my partner and sometimes I play alone. We like to play early in the morning when the crowds are going to work. My partner's name is Franklin and he's from Chile. We've been playing together off and on for about ten years. We play a lot of tunes, as many soft tunes as upbeat rhythms. Even early in the morning, we play high-beat rhythm songs. People like it.

We play some folk tunes from Bolivia, Chile, songs from Peru, and we also play the music we hear on the elevators, stuff like "My Way"–whatever people are conditioned to. I have a lot of cassettes and I listen to a lot of music from other places. Actually, I've been hearing a lot of Celtic songs lately.

As for my children continuing with music, I will certainly offer them an instrument, but I think I would let them find out for themselves what they want to do.

I think Canada has given me the opportunity to live. My wife and I are still a young couple and we have a lot of visions of what we want to do with life. I also went to school here. I studied to be an architectural technologist, but right now there are no possibilities of working in that area. I studied to be the helper of an architect, the one who stands on the side and looks up the laws and the regulations. An architectural technologist gets to draw the doors and the windows instead of the whole house–everything that has to do with building the house.

I want my children to speak French and Spanish. I want them to learn English, too. Some families have the idea that if their children grow up speaking only English, the kids will eventually turn blond or something. Other families feel that they have to

teach Spanish to their kids. Some people are strong in their tradi-
tions; others less so. Some kids play soccer every weekend and
others play baseball. We don't play baseball in our country.

I think most of the friends I have speak Spanish and maintain
it. I don't want my children to be shy of speaking Spanish. I am
proud of being Chilean and my wife is proud of being French.
We are not shy about our cultures.

Claudio Enriquez My name is Claudio Enriquez, I'm twenty-six
years old, and I arrived in Canada when I was close to seven. I'm
studying architecture at Ryerson Polytechnical Institute. I'm doing
my final year. I've already done four years, but I took a year off
to do some travelling, and now I've returned to do my final
thesis. After that, I don't know exactly what I'm going to be
doing. I don't where or for whom I'll be able to work, maybe for
myself. It all depends on the economy.

I remember sequences of our departure from Chile. I have
these vivid pictures that I know are real because I felt them. I've
always felt them and when I went back to those places, it was
true. Many times when I was growing up, I had all these things
in my mind and I didn't really know if they were true or not.
Fragments of memories of places or buildings, and when I went
back, they were all there.

I have a vivid memory of the day that we left. It was like we
were going on a picnic because we packed our bags and we sat
in the back of the car. The lady who took care of the house and
took care of us, too, was there. And our dog–her name was
Susanita–she was a boxer. I can still see them outside the window, behind the car, waving to us as if we were coming back.
That was the last time we saw either of them.

I knew that my father was in trouble because my mother
talked to us very seriously at the time about what was going to
happen. She told us what to say if somebody came up to us and
asked us where our father was. At the time, other families were
being threatened and they were taken away because they told

where their father was or where certain things were locked up in the house. I didn't know about anything like that, we didn't have anything.

The day when the police came to our house to look for my father–I remember there were a lot of them–the first thing I think they did was separate us, take us all into different rooms and question us. I found myself alone with some of them in the garage. One of the soldiers had a machine-gun and was trying to get into all of the boxes and open up all the books and everything in the garage. He was asking me questions about my father. "Where is your father? Where is he?" I remembered that I was not supposed to say anything. At that time, I was six years old. I remember that I kept my cool and didn't say anything. Actually, we really didn't know where he was. My mother never told us where he was. She said that he wasn't home–that was it. They kept opening all the boxes. I told the soldiers that the keys were long gone and they'd never open them. Then they brought us all back to the room. My mother was with someone who must have been the commander, in the backyard, and he was asking her what those holes were in the backyard. My mother said it was the dog, the dog makes holes and buries things. Ordinary things were considered suspicious that day.

I remember when we went to the Canadian embassy, there were hundreds of people. I thought they were cheering us, but now I think they were protesting. I remember they were waving. The bus came and they took my father in the bus. That's all I remember before our departure.

On our way to Canada, my mother was dressing us up in warm clothing because they said it was so cold in Canada. We put on wool hats, wool pants–they were itchy and so hot inside the airplane. We were walking around the airport for hours with the wool hats and scarves. The day we arrived in Canada, it was all white since it had just snowed that day, and it was really cold.

During the second year we were here, my father died of leukaemia. Whenever people tell me how difficult it must have been, I always say it was, but we managed to get through it really well. I had thought that my father only had a cold. We would visit him in the hospital and we were very happy. Nobody ever told us. We didn't know it was serious and that we were never going to see him again. I remember taking all my toys to the hospital and showing him and he could barely understand. It all happened really fast. After he died, we moved to Etobicoke. As children, we had a simple life–we went to school, came back, watched TV, and met with other Chilean families every weekend. My mother had to worry about working and studying. She would always be doing things, trying to get ahead.

I think it was also very tough for my sister, who was the oldest. She had to put up with us.

When we first arrived, we stayed at a hotel on Charles, near Yonge Street. It was a hotel full of refugees. We were always getting blamed for things that other kids were doing. The hotel manager was always mad because there were so many kids running up and down the hallways and making noise. We used to bring in everything we found on the street. We used to find toys, and when we went to a restaurant, they gave us plastic knives and forks, salt and pepper. We used to take home the milk containers. We had a set of cutlery for years, all plastic ware from McDonald's or other stores. Or even used cans from the store, since they were so durable.

When I started school here, I was really shy and I felt so out of place. In Chile, I was in grade one and had just passed to grade two. When I came to Canada, I was placed in grade two and I failed, so they left me in grade two for another year. Then I went to grade three and I failed again, so I had to stay another year. I think I was a bit too young to be in that age group and my English needed improvement.

I don't really remember how I learned the language. My sister understood all the movies on TV, so we would always ask her, "What did he say? What's he talking about?" This was about a year or more after we arrived in Canada. We would sit beside her and she would know exactly what was going on. Apart from school, I guess I learned a lot of English from TV. We went to parties or gatherings every week with other Chileans, so all my friends were Chilean. All my best friends have been Chilean or Latin American ever since I arrived in Canada–even now. When we lived in Old Mill in Etobicoke, there were many Chilean families in that area. The people we used to call Canadians used to call us other things. There was a time when there was a division between the Canadians and the Chileans. These conflicts seemed to be racially motivated and were carried out by a certain group of youths. We were young, but our friends who were much older would always get into fights.

At school, even though my friends were all Canadians, some of their brothers were the ones who were causing all the problems. Inside the school, it was okay, but outside there was so much conflict all the time, just because we were Chilean. It was really difficult for us because my sister had to walk with us everywhere we went. She was always there for us, standing up to the bigger kids.

When we were living in that area, there was a lot of crime. It was terrible. Then after we moved here to the Chilean co-op, everything changed. It was completely different. I started high school and everyone was much nicer and more mature. The new co-op housing was a big improvement from the other building in Old Mill.

It would be difficult to move now because my brother lives next door and my sister is also nearby. Also, my mother has such a close relationship with the kids that if either my brother or sister leaves, it would break up our big family. I like the close structure very much because I can walk from one house to another and visit my nieces and nephews. Not all Chilean families are close. There are many families that want to be separated or are much better off living away from home and relatives. Here, we have the luxury of being very close to each other and still maintaining our privacy.

I went back to Chile in 1987 and stayed for five months. I travelled to northern Chile, where I have an uncle. Then I went to the south of Chile to Valdivia, where I have some friends. I stayed with them for almost a month.

It felt really good going back there, plus it was the first time I travelled outside of Canada. It was all very, very new to me. The first three or four months I was there, I felt like I was learning a lot. My Spanish was improving day by day. I really felt like I wanted to improve more. But after the fifth month, I don't know what happened, I guess I just started missing my own home, my own bed, and by that time I wanted to come back to Canada.

Chile was the same as it was in the postcards, but there were slums and poverty. There is so much misery and hardship for many families. It's hard to tell them that you live in Canada and you have a good life because you feel sorry for them. You just don't want to tell them how great Canada is. At first, I would say how great Canada is and that everyone can study here, but then I didn't want to say anything else because I felt really sorry for a lot of students with whom I had become good friends.

Last December, two of my friends and I bought a Volkswagen van and drove from here to South America. It took us eight months to do the whole trip. At the beginning, we were going to drive four months there and three months back, but the first month we went to Mexico and decided to take it slowly because there was so much to see. We must have visited at least fifteen countries. I just arrived back here in July 1992.

My identity is Chilean. We've always had Chilean music and artefacts at home. I've always felt Chilean. When I went back to Chile the last time, it felt really comfortable going back. I think there will always be a place for me there, but there are still so many problems in Chile. Here in Canada, you can do whatever you want to. If you want to study, you can do it for many years, and you can always travel and come back to Canada and work.

My future is here in Canada. I feel I can be Chilean in Canada. We've always lived in Toronto where there is a high percentage of immigrants and people of foreign nationalities. One way or another, I feel like I belong in this city. It feels good.

I just became a Canadian citizen last year. The first three times I travelled, I used my Chilean passport. People always told me to get my Canadian passport so that I would not get hassled at the borders. So for convenience, I wanted to get my Canadian citizenship before I left on my trip, but I did not receive it until I returned. I think Ontario is really beautiful from what I've seen. It's a great place except for the weather. If Toronto had five months of summer, it would be like paradise. There are so many things to do here in the summer. Every time I go to other countries, I always tell them if they go to Toronto, they should come in the summer because it's beautiful. The atmosphere is really nice. I'm always promoting Toronto wherever I travel.

The next generation in our family will have a new identity–Canadian. Already my niece, Valentina, is always waving her little Canadian flag and sings "O Canada." The new generation won't have too much sentimental attachment to Chile.

My niece speaks Spanish and English. The language is a strong link to our past. Being able to speak both Spanish and English is great because we can travel to so many places and have the option of speaking either language.

The new generation of Chileans gets caught up in the same types of activities that we used to do. Joining soccer clubs and other activities is how they maintain their identity within the Chilean community, but through the new generation, people will become more Canadian. Only through experience can one really separate the hardships of breaking away, from being a refugee. In the beginning, we were a refugee family, but not now.

The Chilean Community

Andrew Israel

O n 11 September 1973, the Chilean people experienced an abrupt and violent change of government. Over the next decade and a half, 24,401 Chilean nationals, mostly refugees, would arrive in Canada. The democratically elected administration of President Salvador Allende was overthrown in a military coup led by General Augusto Pinochet. The bombing of the presidential palace and the assassination of President Allende stunned the world. Pictures of the carnage were reproduced in the world press along with editorial condemnation. But another event, less violent but no less damaging, became a far more significant symbol of the new order that would be established by the Pinochet regime. Soon after the coup, thousands of Chileans were taken from their homes and jobs by the army and locked up in the Santiago soccer stadium, which became a temporary prison. It was a crushing end to the new government that had begun with such high hopes.

After the election of President Allende's Popular Unity government in 1970, Chile had become a model for liberal democratic change. It attracted wide and supportive attention from like-minded people around the world who recognized that land reform and nationalization of strategic industries were essential steps towards a fairer sharing of the country's wealth. But it also attracted the opposition of those with vested interests who had much to lose. The military coup removed both the challenge and the possibility of continuing reform. Those who opposed Allende's leadership and program were not only Chilean nationals.

The new dictatorship clearly feared both popular institutions and the voices of those chosen to lead them. As a result, many groups and individuals among the Chilean intelligentsia became potential enemies of the state and were crushed by the army. Labour unrest and political upheaval gave way to repression and the militarization of civic life. The generals concentrated their attention in the first instance on the removal of known "dissidents"–largely professionals and skilled workers–a process that continued long after the initial 1973 purge.

In addition to members of the Allende government and political activists, the press and other media, union leaders, academics, and students were considered a threat, and large numbers were arrested. Whole faculties of arts and sciences were closed and occupations that were thought to be potentially subversive were banned. Anyone with Marxist or "left-wing" associations was suspect, especially organization and community leaders. Women's groups emerged to play an important role in resisting and publicizing these actions.

Political persecution and human rights violations led many Chileans to flee the country and seek asylum elsewhere. Other Latin American countries, Europe, the United States, Canada, and Australia began to receive a steady flow of refugees. For some time, there was a feeling among many of those who had fled that their exile would be brief and that they would soon return. Some had moved to neighbouring Latin American countries to wait for the change and subsequent recrossing of the border that separated them from home.

The first Chilean refugees arrived in Canada on 9 October 1973, seventeen of the fifty people who found refuge in the Canadian embassy in Santiago. By 26 November, the Canadian government had established a special program for Chileans and, over time, the numbers arriving increased at a steady pace. But administrative constraints reflected a continuing cold war, the hangover of anticommunist sentiment, and Canadian officials were reluctant to admit those considered politically left-wing in 1973.

Public pressure was influential in removing the initial barriers to the Chilean refugees. Some Canadian church groups had had a long-standing connection with Chileans before the coup. A Latin American working group had been established in 1965, and Chilean students in Toronto had received support and an opportunity to exchange views and experience. The Chile Project was established in early 1973, and, the day after the coup, the ad hoc committee on Chile began to lobby Canadian officials. A mix of Canadian and international groups–churches, the UN High Commissioner for Refugees, Chile–Canada solidarity committees, and public gatherings of all kinds–provided the positive pressure that turned the initial positive-but-reluctant Canadian response into a generous and timely opening of the door to people whose lives were endangered and who needed a home.

By the end of 1973, an estimated total of more than 10,000 people had been killed in Chile. By March 1974, approximately 60,000 people were arrested and an estimated 200,000 people lost their jobs for political reasons. Interrogations, long periods of imprisonment without charge or contact with family, and physical and psychological torture became the chief methods of control. General Pinochet had declared a state of siege, claiming the need for the government to defend itself by whatever means necessary. Eventually the state of siege was replaced by a state of emergency that was meant to reflect the achievement of some stability and order, but the regime continued to defend itself with guns and tanks, and with laws that set aside the rule of law and civil rights.

Although a large percentage of Chilean refugees came to Canada with good education, skills, and professional training, many were unable to find work in their professions or trades. Others found work, but far below their professional qualifications; they experienced a severe loss of income and social status. In Chile, their sense of personal worth and status had been significantly influenced by the nature of their jobs. In Canada, the decline in status made adapting to their new home more difficult.

Chileans enjoy a tradition of large extended families, often living in one house with a recognized hierarchy that establishes the senior father and husband as the dominant decision-maker. In

Canada, a range of family and gender-based relationships had to be renegotiated. The problem with a man's loss of status at work was aggravated by changes in the traditional role of women. The wife and mother, who in Chile had rarely worked outside the home, in Canada had a job in the workplace to help support the family, along with a concomitant increase in status and freedom.

Chileans are evenly distributed throughout major urban centres in Canada, in contrast to many other immigrant/refugee groups that concentrated in Toronto and Montreal. In Toronto, the Bathurst/College and Jane/Finch/Weston Road areas represent the conglomerates of the Chilean community. The community is united by bonds of culture and political ideology that provide the basis for social interaction. The desire to preserve their cultural heritage is demonstrated through many cultural and arts activities.

Local community organizations provide essential services to the community. Chileans were the first Spanish-speaking group to resettle in Canada in any significant numbers. Upon their arrival, there were no services, agencies, or resources to meet their specific needs. Subsequently, the Chilean refugees established their own Spanish-speaking social service organizations that paved the way for later waves of South and Central American refugees. Today, a highly developed network of community, social, health, sports, and women's and children's organizations are available to help newcomers adapt to Canada.

Founded by Chileans in 1973, the Centre for Spanish-Speaking Peoples recently celebrated its twentieth anniversary. It helps Spanish-speaking refugees and immigrants with problems they may have upon arrival in Canada, and provides counselling, ESL classes, and legal, health, and family advice. Other early organizations included the Toronto Chilean Association and the Toronto Chile Society which maintained awareness of the socio-political situation in Chile. As most of the refugees left because of their political pursuits, a keen interest in politics at home is maintained through panel discussions and Chilean current affairs forums.

Formally, Chile has been restored to its democratic standing.

In reality, democratization is a gradual process that many Chileans feel will not be complete until the military is accountable to the elected government. The government of Chile, meanwhile, has sent formal notice that it welcomes the return of those who fled in the 1970s. Chileans in Canada now face a new challenge: whether or not to uproot themselves once more and move back to Chile. The problem is made more poignant by the rootedness that their children, now grown, may feel in Canada and the children's reluctance to return to a country they knew only to visit. The older generation–now grandparents themselves–frequently find that the Chile they are now free to visit and resettle is not the Chile they left. Many find that Canada is, in the final analysis, their home.

References

Allodi, A. and A. Rojas. "The Role of a Housing Cooperative Community in the Mental Health and Social Adaptation of Latin American Refugees in Toronto," *Migration World*, Vol. XVI, No. 3 (Staten Island, N.Y., 1988), pp. 17-21.

Mata, F.G. *The Four Immigrant Waves from Latin America to Canada: Historical, Demographic and Social Profiles* (Toron-to: Centre for Refugee Studies, 1985).

Rockhill, K., and P. Tomic. *Accessing ESL: An Exploration into the Effects of Institutionalized Racism and Sexism in Shaping the Lives of Latin American Immigrant and Refugee Women in Metropolitan Toronto* (Toronto: Ontario Institute for Studies in Education, 1992).

Rodas, R.E. *No More Children of a Postponed Dream* (Toronto: Hispanic Council of Metropolitan Toronto, 1993).

Simalchik, Joan. "Part of the Awakening: Canadian Churches Respond to Chile 1970-73." Unpublished manuscript (Toronto: Multicultural History Society of Ontario, n.d.).

Vietnamese

The Pham Family

Jennifer Khong

In 1979, when the horrifying images of Vietnamese refugees who were fleeing from the violence and desperation under communist rule and boarding shaky boats to cross the South China Sea were shown on TV, thousands of ordinary Canadians from across the country responded and opened their arms and hearts to welcome and help those who made it to the other side of the sea. Many of these Vietnamese refugees, who were also known as the boat people, have since rebuilt their homes and community in Canada. Pham, Thê Trung and his wife Thai, Ni Phan, are two of them.

Pham was a graduate of Saigon National University of Art when South Vietnam fell into the hands of the North Vietnamese communist regime in 1975. The communists introduced an agricultural revolution, seizing–often violently–privately held lands and converting them to state ownership. Many resisted and faced harsh repercussions, even death. Pham's parents were originally farmers in the Mekong Delta, forced by war to relocate earlier to Saigon. As a young art graduate, and then single, Pham was assigned a job by the state, drawing propaganda posters for the Vietnamese government to protest the conflicts along the border between Vietnam and China.

Because of his job, Pham often had to travel away from his family. Military draft was imminent. On the eve of the Vietnamese *Tet* (New Year) in 1980, Pham decided to escape from the oppression he was suffering. He and his youngest brother, the two youngest of seven children, left their family after the New Year's Eve family dinner to search for freedom.

11. Pham, Thê Trung carrying his only remaining possession–his artist's satchel–with a friend in the Songkhla Refugee Camp, Thailand, 1980 (Photo: courtesy of the Pham family)

For Pham and his brother, it was the beginning of a five-month long journey to freedom. They boarded a 10-metre long wooden boat at Ca Mau, the most southern point of South Vietnam. The boat carried about fifty-nine people, including the elderly, young men, and women with small children. The boat met with a terrifying storm, which destroyed the gas tank. The boat went off course and was later seized by a North Vietnamese navy patrol while sailing towards international waters. All the passengers were subjected to intimidation by the patrol and threatened with imprisonment. The crew and passengers decided to offer as bribes the few belongings they had brought with them on the journey.

After two days of negotiation, the soldiers took the bribes and let them go. Later, they encountered merchant sailors who were willing to supply them with some oil and food from their own ship stock, but who refused to rescue them. As they journeyed on, they were attacked by a Thai pirate ship that tried to rob them, only to find that the passengers had nothing left to steal. The pirates then informed the crew that the boat was going the wrong way. Recharting their course, the vessel slowly made its way to the shores of Thailand. The exhausted and starving passengers and crew were sent to the Songkhla Refugee Camp.

While Pham waited in the refugee camp to be processed and resettled in a third country, he took every opportunity he had to create and capture his traumatic experience through his art. Conditions in the Songkhla Refugee Camp were extremely cramped and inadequate for the population of boat people it sheltered. Pham lived under a tree in a hammock and stayed in the camp from February to early June. When the opportunity arose for him to apply for permanent asylum, he chose Canada. In June 1980, Pham arrived in Canada under the government-sponsored category. Pham and his brother left Bangkok and flew to Montreal, and then to London, Ontario. From London they were driven to Stratford by the Canadian family that sponsored them, John and Grace Gilbert.

While living in Stratford, Pham also received a great deal of support from local Canadians and the church he attended. In 1982, he decided to relocate to Toronto in hopes of finding work and joining the Vietnamese community. He received assistance from the Vietnamese Association of Toronto and caring Torontonians who were total strangers to him. Pham started his first job in Georgetown as an assistant in finishing art products.

In 1983, Pham was able to reconnect with his girlfriend, Thai, who by then had fled to France with her family. In 1984, he flew to Paris to marry her and they both decided to build their new home in Toronto. The couple's romance is unique and is a wartime love story. Their love for each other has outlived physical separation of thousands of miles and limited communication. Thai tried to escape by boat three times, but failed. Her brother eventually sponsored her to go to France in 1983. Once in Paris, she wrote to Pham who called her and proposed.

Thai, who majored in biology at Saigon University, originally intended to pursue her studies in the medical field. Under the communist regime in Vietnam, she had also been trained in fashion design and traditional craft work. After her arrival in Toronto, Thai worked as a sewing operator for a fashion manufacturer during the day and did her own fashion design work in the evening to make ends meet. She also wanted to save enough money to sponsor the rest of her family to come to Canada. Both Pham and Thai worked extremely hard to support themselves and the rest of their family.

In 1986, Thai was able to reunite with her parents. In the same year that their first child, Daniel (Hieu), was born, Thai started her own fashion design boutique.

After working for an art foundry industry for several years, Pham opened his own custom plaster studio. He produces and designs a variety of things, such as cornices, panel mouldings, ceiling decorations, and elaborate murals. In May 1993, Pham competed with international artists and was commissioned to do a bronze statue entitled, "Escaped to Freedom." This project is co-sponsored by the Vietnamese Federation Association in Canada (Capital Region) and the City of Ottawa. This bronze statue is expected to be completed in 1994 and will be located at Preston Avenue and Somerset Road in Ottawa.

To this day, Pham still has the only possession from his old life that he was able to save–a leather artist's satchel on which he printed in white letters his refugee identification number from the Songkhla Refugee Camp. He keeps the satchel in order to bequeath it eventually to his son, Hieu, so that he will not forget the great danger and sacrifices his father endured in seeking freedom and a new life.

In May 1993, after this interview, the Phams had their second child, David (Hai).

The Pham Family Speaks

Interviewed by Jennifer Khong

P ham, Thê Trung I lived in Vietnam and worked with the communist regime until 1980. During that time, I was in art college. In 1978, I graduated and they sent me to work in a small town south of Saigon.

We had to travel about one day's drive. I felt so depressed. I had no freedom. In 1979, my family was still in Saigon and I lived by myself. I was single. I decided to escape in 1975, but I didn't have a chance to escape because I had to work to survive. As I wanted to live by myself, it was hard, so I had to get along with the government, who gave me a job. I had to work with them for three years, but I am an artist and I want to do it my way–in freedom. If you don't have freedom, you cannot create things. That's the reason I decided to escape.

One day I went back to Saigon and I told my family, my mother and father. It was New Year's Eve. I remember that night. We had dinner together. At about five o'clock in the morning, we organized. I said I have to escape by boat. I was going to the border and organizing fifty-nine people to go by boat in the direction of Thailand. Heading for Thailand was the shortest way to cross the ocean.

The boat was about 10 metres long and about 4 wide. There were children, maybe five of them, and mostly young people. There were five or six couples and some single young men.

We took about five days to cross the sea from Vietnam to Thailand and we had lots of things happening on the trip.

The first day I went to the town named Ca Mau. We left like the fishermen. There were fifty-nine people in the boat. Over the top of the boat, we had some net, like fishing net. The fishermen on the boat went fishing every day, so they had permission, they would be okay. But this time, they were hiding fifty-nine people under the boat, covered by fishing net, so no one would notice. We were lucky the first day when we came to where the river met the sea. There were big waves in the sea and lots of people got seasick.

We brought food and water, but there was not enough for our whole trip, so we tried to save. On the way, we got lost. Instead of going straight to Thailand, the waves and storm pushed the boat near Kampuchea. We didn't know that, we thought we were on the way to Thailand.

The waves and storm pushed us far, but we were unlucky and met the communist patrol ship. They captured us and they shot the boat because we were still running, we didn't stop. One hour later, the boat had to stop because one bullet got through the boat. It started leaking and the oil came out from the gas tank. We had no more oil and then we could not run it any more, but we were lucky that no one got hurt.

The patrol ship followed and tried to approach closer. We stopped, then they jumped and captured us. They took us back to Vietnam. We were tied up in the back. That night I remember it was raining. You could move a little bit, but they tied your hands so that you could not take any action. That night was so rainy and dark. I could see a thunderstorm and it looked very scary. The people were suffering. With the dark storm and the rain we were outside and it was cold. We thought maybe in a couple of days we will go to jail and somebody will get killed. We didn't know, we couldn't imagine. But I was okay. We could do nothing. But early in the morning, some communist sailors came over and they said that tomorrow we will be back in Vietnam where we left. All of us will go to jail or get killed. They said it like that.

I felt very bad, I felt unfortunate. I felt the future was very dark. I wanted to know what was going on. I was with my younger brother. I was twenty-three and he was only eighteen.

I remember I was with people of religions different from my own. I am Protestant. People were Catholic or Buddhist and they prayed. The only thing that you can do is pray because nothing is in your power, you can't do anything. So people prayed. No one can help you on the ocean between the sky and the water, so we prayed. I knew one or two people would get killed, and all of us might go to jail. At that time, it was very serious, not very easy.

There was no reason for the patrol to release us, but we thought of a way we might get them to do it. We could take off everything we brought along–jewellery, money, anything, our clothes. We could give them everything and they could release us. The patrol said no, they didn't want to. We bargained with them. After one day, they were still thinking how they could make the deal with us. They checked everything. We said we had some gold and jewellery. One day they said okay, they can do it, and we shouldn't tell. The communists want something for themselves all the time. They don't want to say anything. They said if they release us, we shouldn't tell anyone it was their ship that released us and we said okay, let us go and we will try the trip. They released us. We gave them everything. And we had a chance to go like that.

Another challenge. We had to go again, start again, only now we didn't have anything. There was not much oil, but we fixed the engine, and we tried to fill some holes and just go slowly and try to get out of there.

The second day on the ocean, we met a merchant ship, and they gave us some oil and food. They wouldn't rescue us up because there were so many people. They said our boat was still okay. We tried to go on. We met pirates. They tried to capture us, but we didn't have anything. We had given everything to the communist ship already. We tried to go slowly, and in the end we got to Thailand, but before that, we were captured many times. They took the women away. We were hungry, but we still had something, we were still lucky.

When we got to Thailand, some of the passengers were sick, but we were okay. We had been together for five days. We were still all right. The boat was broken, it sank in the water. We saw on the ocean lots of things floating–a piece of wood, maybe from another boat, a woman's hat, and a blanket. And bags, luggage, clothes–all on the ocean. I cried to myself. I saw somebody dying. I felt bad. When I was on the ocean, in the morning I would sit at the front and watch the sun rise, up high at noon, and then go down at sunset. Every day I did that. I counted so I remembered it was five days.

I didn't know about the future. I just hoped. I saw the sun rise in front of me, and I saw the sun set in back of me. I never knew what would happen in the future.

When I escaped, I never told Ni Phan my plans because everything had to be kept secret from everyone, even your relatives, so I never told anybody. On the way, if you get captured by the communists, you get in lots of trouble. And if my relatives and friends know, maybe the communists will capture them, so I didn't want anybody to have problems if I was unsuccessful. But when I got to Thailand, I sent a telegram to my brother in Japan, and my brother sent it to Vietnam. Then they knew and said I was lucky. Then my girlfriend knew I was in Thailand.

When you go out into the ocean, you cannot do anything. You have just the water and the sky. If there was a big storm, you just pray. Only God can help people when they get between life and death. You never know.

The Thai police control saw us from far away. They came over and we had a white flag, the rescue SOS flag. They said we were refugees from Vietnam. We followed them and landed in Songkhla, where they had a big camp. They got information from us in one night, and they fed fifty-nine people through the Thai Red Cross. They gave us food to eat that night.

They knew we were hungry and tired. They phoned the refugee camp and we travelled about a half hour more. They brought the bus to pick us up and deliver us to the camp. At that time, I think there were about 15,000 people in the camp. They welcomed us and they came over and held hands and we were united. I think we were there for five months. I got an interview with the Canadian embassy and applied for immigration to Canada.

When I was in Vietnam, I decided that when I go to another country, I would choose Canada. I like Canada because of the kindness of the people, and the country can support and help lots of countries around the world. I like Canada because they don't get involved with lots of war or politics. People are kind, they give help to people who want to develop. That's the reason, and I was curious. Canada is at the top of North America. I was curious, I wanted to travel. Maybe in the future, I could get a passport and go to the United States or Europe. I feel in that way it's very good and very fine for me.

I escaped. It was not like going on holidays. You go on this kind of trip to escape. I had to be careful to avoid accidents. Pirates came and you have to take care of yourself, but when everything was quiet, my soul needed to rest. When I looked at people dying in the ocean or something else I saw, I thought should record it and keep it in my mind, so when I have a chance to write, I can tell the story, or I can paint it, or I can do my art through my experience. So I was really careful to watch everything around me, to record everything.

When I arrived at the refugee camp, I started to do something. Every day I took paper to sketch. I wanted to keep it like a diary, so I went around the camp and painted and drew every day. I made about fifty drawings and sketches by ink and water-colour. People organized an exhibit for my art and they came and enjoyed it and some people bought. This was at the camp, but the Vietnamese did not buy. The people who worked at the camp came–people from the United States and Europe and Canadian people. They came over to help people. They bought my paintings. I was happy because they wanted to help me and I had something for them.

If people were interested in my work, I would sketch their portrait for them as a souvenir. There were lots of people from the churches, Catholic and Protestant. I met lots of young people who were volunteers. They said they wanted to help. I had the chance to speak and learn English there. I made one or two friends there. One was from England, one was from Holland, and one was Canadian.

I met a minister of the Mennonite church in Canada. He used to work in the refugee camp, but now he is in Winnipeg. He is a very kind man. I remember he took me to get permission from the Thai camp security and he sponsored me for one day to travel to Bangkok, so I could enjoy freedom for one day. He took me by taxi and showed me the museum. He showed me the royal murals and the temples–beautiful. That was one day for me in Bangkok, and then I came back to the camp.

Some people there knew English and they could teach or you could learn some geography of the country where you were going–Canada's geography, population, religion, culture, how many people live there, the provinces. That's how you have to do it. You have to be ready to learn it and go to one of the countries you choose.

I was surprised when I was first directed to Montreal. I have only one relative in Canada. He is my cousin, a pharmacist. I got in touch with him by mail. I told the embassy officer that the only place I have relatives is in Saskatoon, Saskatchewan. I thought I would go to live close to him in Saskatchewan, but I was surprised when I was sent to Montreal.

They can send people everywhere. Some people go to Edmonton, Vancouver, Halifax, Toronto, everywhere. When they interviewed me again, they asked me if I wanted to live in Ontario. I said I don't care, I am happy with this land that I chose. You send me to Toronto, anywhere, I don't know. They asked me about my occupation. I said I work as an artist, so I can go somewhere suited to me. They said okay and sent me to Stratford, Ontario. He said Stratford might be good for me. I don't know how. I came over here. Stratford is the name of the village where Shakespeare was born in England. That is a very beautiful place–romantic. I came here to live–very nice.

I had an older brother who lived in Japan. I didn't want to write a letter directly to Vietnam. At that time, the communists were very serious. If there were any problems with the politics, it could still involve my family in Vietnam, so I wrote letters to my brother in Japan, and he wrote to Vietnam. From Japan to Vietnam would be okay, but not from Canada or the United States. I used to do that.

I was government sponsored. In Stratford the first year, some people came to help and they rented the apartment. The government helped to show me how to live, what the apartment looked like, everything in the town.

We rested about one month. We had government applications for OHIP, social insurance numbers, everything for a landed immigrant. Then in the summertime, in June, there were ESL classes, English as a second language. We went there until Christmas, six months. I still worked. I started to work with ink drawings, and I made some artwork to show at the gallery in Stratford. That was two months after I arrived in Stratford. I brought about fifty sketches from the refugee camp, and I showed them to the community at Stratford.

At that time, it was the Stratford Festival. The local church I attended helped me to arrange a show there and frame my work. And maybe I could sell. They appreciated my work. Lots of people came to buy. They helped me make a better life. I don't make lots of money. At that time, I had about $400 or $500, so I was happy. That was a lot of money for me at that time. I connected with some people in town and they wanted to have something special, so I painted some things in their house. I painted some portraits and made some money.

After I finished school there a year later, I wanted to go work in a bigger city, so I connected with some of my friends in Toronto. The Vietnamese community in Toronto is bigger now and I wanted to join the Vietnamese community, so I left Stratford.

When I first arrived in Montreal and Stratford, I was surprised a little bit, but not very much because in Saigon I used to learn art and I read lots of western books about art or geography, or *Reader's Digest*. I knew what Canada, the United States, and France looked like. I could imagine. The buildings are higher, and there are more cars, traffic, lots of traffic here, the highway is busy. The country is different. Life is faster, and you travel, and you have to follow the law and everything. At that time, I didn't go very far, but I saw everything. I feel very comfortable.

The first winter, it was really cold. You can see the snow you dreamed of, you can see how Christmas is. In Saigon, if you are Christian, you go to church, but you cannot enjoy Christmas like in Canada. They don't like religion to get involved with the communist politics.

In Saigon, many churches were closed, but some small churches are still open illegally. There were about fifty or one hundred people meeting. If the village or town communist officer says you are not allowed to organize a meeting, you have to go away. When you get permission, you could have a Christmas celebration.

In Canada, I find that every community is very proud of its culture. In Canada, they welcome all. You can wear your own costumes. In Vietnam, if you work for the government, you can only wear one uniform, all in one colour. Also, you have to eat the same food as the others. That's the way you have it. You line up to get food every day. But here you are free, you work hard, you get some money, you save money, you can buy a house. If you don't have lots of money, you still get enough food.

Once we were in Canada, I lived with my younger brother for about five years until 1985. He was eighteen, I was twenty-three when we arrived. I just had two brothers in Canada. I had to raise him. When I had money, I worked and we lived together in the same apartment. He used to go to high school. After a few years,

12. Pham, Thê Trung in Artmaster Studio, his own business which produces custom plaster mouldings for Toronto homes, 1993 (Photo: Vincenzo Pietropaolo)

he got into McMaster University in Hamilton. He has some money for himself and he started to learn engineering, his career. I am happy that he is successful. He became a professional engineer. He works with a good company.

I was writing to Ni Phan, my girlfriend, saying that any time she was out of the country, any country, I will go to see her and sponsor her. I was serious about my commitment and my promise. I thought she was in China, Thailand, Malaysia, or Hong Kong. I never knew she was in France because the French could not receive any more refugees.

In 1985, I got news from Ni Phan by mail from France. She had landed in France in 1985 and was united with her family. We communicated for three or five months. Finally, I went over there and we got married in Paris. We were separated for a long time and then met again. It was like I was born again in the ocean–I almost died and someone saved me. We decided to return to

Canada. We lived in a small apartment. My brother at that time lived in an apartment in Hamilton because he was studying.

My older brothers and sisters whom we sponsored to join us adapted to life in Canada more slowly. The younger ones can join the community easier because they have more time and an open mind. The older ones want to work right away–any kind of work, so it is very difficult since they try to do something they have no experience in. They work in labour and they get paid by the hour. My sister can use a sewing machine. The first month they get tired because they are not used to it.

There was lots of work here. I connected with the Vietnamese community. They showed me how to do any kind of work to make money to raise my brother and myself. If I can save some money, I can send some to help my family in Vietnam. So the first day I went to see the Vietnamese Association. I saw people and they asked me what my occupation was in Vietnam. I said I used to do art in advertising or sculptures. I graduated from the University of Art in Saigon. They showed me the Yellow Pages. So I took a map and went door to door and asked for jobs. One day I stopped by a gallery and an artist helped me. They phoned the Art Cast Company in Georgetown. They cast bronze sculpture you see around the city. They said to send him in tomorrow. He showed me how to get there. It was so far away and I went by train. If he accepted me, I can work for him and rent an apartment there and stay, so no problem.

When my mother came here, she was a little disappointed at first about the culture, the neighbourhood, the situation in Canada because she has no English. My wife and I worked all day, so she was very lonely. She cried. Many times, she said that she wanted to go home, but after one year, she was okay. She has friends and tries to speak to them on the telephone. She is all right, she is happy for now. My mother is seventy-one years old. My father is the same age and he is still working, helping my brother back in Vietnam with the business.

Thai, Ni Phan In 1975, I was still studying biology at the university. At that time I met Pham and we had a great friendship. Besides that, I learned fashion design because I am interested.

My family is quite big. My parents have seven children. One sister and one brother got married and they have two children each. I lived with my parents.

Pham asked me to escape with him in 1980. In 1979, I had tried already to leave Vietnam by boat. My family paid a lot of gold. We tried three times. That's why I didn't want to go with him.

When I left my country for the first time, I tried to go by boat, thinking it was like an adventure, going to some other place where you can have freedom to live. Under the communists, everything is very disciplined. I was really interested in biology. After I graduated, I thought I could go somewhere and do something else. I never thought I would meet Pham again. I was very surprised.

The Chinese and the Vietnamese live with their families. You think that is okay in your country. Here you have many chances to develop your skills. In Vietnam, after you graduate from university, you have to work for the government for at least two years and do whatever they want if you want to get the certificate. They wanted me to go to a rural area, and we were already living in the capital. I didn't want to leave my family to go to a really small town far away. We tried to get some place in Saigon, but they didn't allow it. They only allow people who have good connections with the communist government.

When I escaped, I went with my sister, my brother-in-law, their children, and some other relatives. It didn't work and we lost a lot of money. I tried to go by boat three times. I got robbed by a pirate on the sea on the way to Thailand. That pirate boat was small. They had about six or seven people.

Our boat was about 15 metres, with about 150 people. The pirates took the jewellery, the gold, and then they let us go because there were too many people. The boat was damaged, and they took everything. When we started the boat, something was wrong. We fixed the boat and went on for a few hours. After we fixed it a second time, there was a storm and we had to wait. Then we had to come back.

By that time, we didn't know if we should go back to the place where we started, but the owner of the boat wanted to try again because they had a lot of gold they put in the boat, because they had a big family. They wanted to fix the boat and go on again. When the boat was damaged again, we had to stop and everybody had to jump in the ocean and swim to the shore. I think it was about 2 kilometres. Many children had to be carried on adults' shoulders. They kept us in one area. We were not allowed to go out because they were afraid that people would find out that we tried to escape. By the time they were ready to go again, I was disappointed and I didn't want to go again.

The government used to turn a blind eye and allow some people to escape, but then they stopped it. Many other people tried to escape by boat. Some of them got lost. My aunt's two sons left in 1978. They never came back and they never heard any news of them until now. They have two older sons and they may be down in the ocean.

By 1980, I was just graduating from university. I didn't want to work for the communist government, so I just stayed home and worked in fashion design. I had my own business. Then I taught in the fashion school.

My school was close to Pham's house, so I passed by sometimes and got news of him. A few weeks after he left, his family got a letter and they let me know that he was already in a refugee camp in Thailand. His family said he was really sad and expecting a letter from me, so I tried to write him a letter. When he went to Canada, I got some letters and I wrote him. I got some news from his family sometimes.

I decided to stay in Vietnam until the day we got a letter from the French consulate. They called me and my sister for the health exam and gave us a visa to get to France. My brother was here and he sponsored the whole family, but nobody left because the French government refused. My brother had someone help him and he gave my name and my sister's name. He had a very good teacher and she knew somebody in the government in France. They said that they can sponsor two people. We were already refused and had no chance to go until 1983.

I taught a few hours a day and worked at home making dresses and suits for customers. I also like to do other work like crochet. Everybody is interested and they said I could sell them and then I tried.

In 1975, when the communists came, they asked everybody to change their money. My family had only $200. If you had a lot of money, you put it in the bank and you are not allowed to take it out. Because we had two families, we were allowed to change $400. By that time, I stayed at home and I was very sad. I crocheted nice things for children. Everybody said they were very nice and then all the friends wanted to buy them. I sold them and made a living.

Pham sent me some pictures. He was very lonely. My brother in France had a family and one child. He lived in a small town. I lived there for a few months after I moved.

It was very hard to afford my own apartment, so I moved about 20 km away with my sister. When I first arrived in France, I wrote Pham a letter, just like I wrote all my friends, and in the letter I put my telephone number. When he got the letter, he phoned me.

I was so surprised. It was two or three o'clock in the morning. I was so surprised–I thought I would never meet him again, but hearing his voice made him seem so close. Pham said that he would come at Christmas in 1983, and he asked me to marry him. We got married in January 1984. We have just had our ninth anniversary.

He told me Canada is easy to live in. He had a job, and anyway, the wife has to follow the husband. That is our culture I had planned to continue with medicine in France, and I thought

13. Pham, Thê Trung and Thai, Ni Phan are reunited and married in Paris, 1984 (Photo: courtesy of the Pham family)

14. Thai, Ni Phan in her Toronto dress shop, Thoi Trang, two weeks before her second child was born, 1993 (Photo: Vincenzo Pietropaolo)

I could continue here in Canada, but everything is not like what you want. When we came here, we started a business and the business was quite good.

I worked in a factory for a while to sponsor my family. He sponsored his own family. This was in May 1984. I worked for eight hours every day in the factory. When I went home, I worked on my own business because I got customers easily day by day.

I sponsored my whole family, but my parents came first. My husband and I sponsored everybody, a total of thirteen people. We worked hard. All my sisters and brothers were already over twenty-one years old. They could not come at that time. My mother was a housewife back home. She liked being a housewife, cooking, taking care of the house. When she went to Chinatown, she asked about jobs in the supermarket. They need people who could cook for employees in the supermarket. She got that job and still has it. Already six years in one place. She really enjoyed that job. She is sixty-three. Maybe she will retire soon. My father is much older than my mother. When he came here, he was already almost eighty. Now he is eighty-three. He is still working for a Chinese association.

At the beginning, it was a little hard for my parents because of the language and customs. Usually we worked too many hours and didn't have much time for them. They were a little bit disappointed. But after a few months when my mother found a job, she was happy. My father goes to Chinatown. He has a lot of friends because he was a teacher and has a lot of students living here in Canada. They have a Chinese association and they need people who can write nice Chinese letters and take care of the paperwork. They asked my father and he said he would help them, not for money, just for fun. They paid him a few hundred a month, and he was enjoying it, so he worked for more than two years. The association didn't have enough money. They asked my father to work, but didn't pay. This was about four years ago. By

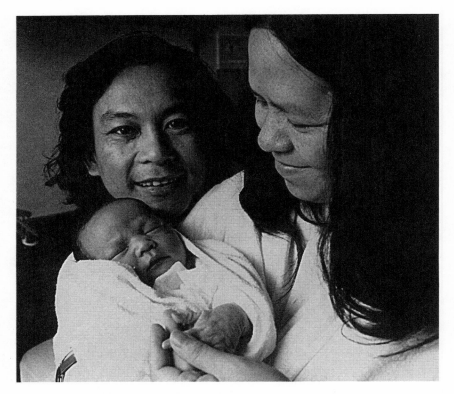

15. Pham, Thê Trung and Thai, Ni Phan with their newborn son, Hai (David), Toronto 1993 (Photo: Vincenzo Pietropaolo)

that time, my father was having problems with his eye. He has glaucoma that started in Vietnam a long time ago. When he went to the hospital, they said it was a cataract. They tried surgery many times. It is a little bit better, but day by day, he is getting older and he does not have good vision. He decided to stop working for the association.

He likes reading and writing. I think it is no problem for him. My parents are now living with my sister and brother. I don't have to worry too much because someone can take care of them. Before I had to take care of them. I can phone them about every two days or whenever I need to. It is not so far to visit, so we can go whenever we want.

When my parents came, I worked in my own business. At the beginning, we had to work for somebody else to get some experience. For any job, you keep learning and practising. Even now in my own business, I keep learning. After almost two years, I learned a lot from the factory. Most of my customers are from this area, and many old customers bring new customers whenever they are looking for a good tailor. They know what you have worked on already, and they bring other people.

I work for all kinds of customers—Italian, Portuguese, Greek, Ukrainian. I have Vietnamese customers, too. I had about three assistants here with me and another two at home. Each one worked on one thing.

I am expecting our second child the first week in May. Sometimes I feel very tired and sometimes I feel okay. I'm lucky that I have good health, so it is not so bad right now. We really enjoy our family, and we are very happy with the child we have. That's why we are having another one.

The Vietnamese Community

Jennifer Khong

The Vietnamese have settled in Toronto in three distinct periods in the last two decades. Between 1950–75, there were a handful of Vietnamese students and professionals who were either in the process of completing their studies or who chose to stay after graduating. Between April 1975 and the end of 1978, the first group of Vietnamese refugees, who arrived after the North Vietnamese communist regime seized the Republic of South Vietnam, numbered 1,500 in Ontario and 1,000 in Metro Toronto.[1]

In 1979, Canada decided to accept 50,000 Indochinese refugees, who were also known as the boat people. Approximately 300,000 died–they were drowned, starved, or murdered in their flight to freedom.[2] By 1980, about 2,000 had arrived in Metro Toronto. By 1982, the number grew to 12,000. Between 1983 and 1986, this population expanded to 30,000 largely through secondary migration.[3]

Like most immigrants, the majority of the Vietnamese settled in predominantly urban settings, such as Montreal, Vancouver, Edmonton, Calgary, Winnipeg, and Toronto. Toronto has the highest concentration of Vietnamese in Canada. This population can be further identified as roughly 70 per cent of ethnic Vietnamese origin and 30 per cent Vietnamese of Chinese origin.[4] In the 1986 census, the number of people in Canada who were born in Vietnam was 82,760, of which 32,255 resided in Ontario. In the 1991 census data, the total population had risen to 113,595 in Canada, of which 51,025.[5] resided in Ontario. The 1991 census also indicated that in Metro Toronto, 20,170 of this population identified their ethnic origin as Vietnamese.[6]

Except for those who arrived prior to 1975, the Vietnamese refugees and immigrants obtained their status of entry under family unification, non-government, or government sponsorship.[7]

The majority of the Toronto Vietnamese have settled in several downtown areas: Bloor Street and Jane, bounded by the Humber River on the west and Dundas on the north; between Dufferin and Bathurst, from St Clair Avenue north to Eglinton; and north of Eglinton between Keele and Dufferin. Other pockets are scattered in different areas in Metro Toronto and York Region. In the last few years, there has been a gradual increase of the Vietnamese presence in Mississauga.[8]

Currently in Metro Toronto, including Mississauga, there are thirty Vietnamese-speaking physicians, seventeen dentists, eighteen pharmacies with Vietnamese pharmacists, nineteen real estate agents, and seventeen insurance brokers. There are eleven journals and magazines and nine publishers. The Vietnamese business community persists in the face of the recession.

A leading social service organization is the Vietnamese Association of Toronto, which was established in 1972 to serve the rapidly increasing numbers of Vietnamese immigrants. There are now twenty-five social and cultural associations, including a university Vietnamese-Canadian students group, and a Society of Vietnamese-Canadian Professionals. All these reflect the professional training and background of many and the emphasis placed on education and culture within the Vietnamese community.

Of paramount importance are the nine temples, one Catholic church, and six Protestant churches that serve the Vietnamese. The two major religions of the Vietnamese community are Buddhism and Christianity. Many Vietnamese continue the traditional practice of ancestor worship. Other religions include Hoa Hao and Cao Dai (which combine elements of Catholicism, Buddhism, and Taoism).[9]

Vietnamese culture has been deeply influenced by Taoism, Confucianism, and Buddhism.[10] Taoism seeks to define a place for humans in relation to the universe and teaches them to keep in harmony with the environment.[11] Confucianism provides people with an ethical code of conduct in relation to their society.[12] According to Buddhism, people can influence the course of their destiny: by suppressing all desires that tie them to this earth, people can free themselves from reincarnation and become like Buddha, an all-knowing, compassionate, and smiling divinity.[13]

The Taoist concept of harmony plays a significant role in the Vietnamese system of values. Keeping harmony in life means understanding that everything is relative and nothing is absolute. Therefore, a reasonable person should not worry if a preferred solution to a problem is no longer possible. Under this influence, the Vietnamese accept a pluralistic approach to life, which emphasizes a constant search for alternatives. Taoists believe that the laws of the universe and nature cannot be changed. As humans, we should not try to change the environment, but rather blend into it and do the best we can under the circumstances.

Confucianism is concerned with politics and human ethics, and with keeping harmony in society while aiming to perfect humans, considered the keystone of society. As humans, we are the principal agent of both harmony and disharmony in society.

The basic social unit of the Confucian system is the well-ordered family, which is the cornerstone of the socio-political order. Everyone has a clearly defined role and a recognized rank in society and the family. The Confucian principle of filial piety is alive and well in many Vietnamese households where there are closely knit extended families. Usually there are three generations living under the same roof. This living arrangement is considered evidence of "a blessed house" because the children are fulfilling their filial duties in caring for the elderly.[14]

Confucianism encourages upward mobility through diligence and knowledge. Under this influence, the Vietnamese develop *tanh hieu hoc*, a deep respect for the learned and their knowledge.[15] There has been, however, criticism about the passive and reserved behaviour of many Vietnamese students. Taoism appreciates inaction and placidity.[16] Vietnamese students demonstrate Taoist characteristics by being inactive, quiet, and not asking questions in class even when they do not understand. They do, however, answer questions directed to them. Talking when they do not have to means preventing another student or the teacher from talking. This could be disturbing and impolite, while talking when they are asked to do so would not be disturbing to others.

In Toronto, there are 1,248 elementary students of Vietnamese origin, and 2,700 registered in secondary schools. Over two-thirds of the high school students complete the high school program on schedule, which is a higher rate compared to the 50 per cent rate of the average Toronto student population.

When asked to comment on the major characteristics of their people, many Vietnamese mention *tanh can cu*, which means the silent willingness to do things the hard way when it is the only way possible.[17] This source of strength is reflected in the courageous escape from Vietnam that so many undertook. It is also reflected in the achievements of this new community in Canada within such a short time and with so few resources available at the time of their arrival. In their search for political freedom, the boat people chose to risk their lives to escape from communist rule.

Dr David Bai, a political anthropologist at the University of Alberta and past chairman of the Edmonton Immigrant Services Association, has observed, "To be Vietnamese is to be used to struggle.... We need to bear in mind that these are people with a tremendous will to overcome hardship. As such, they are the kind of people who can contribute a great deal to the strength of this country."[18]

Notes

1. "Indochinese Refugees," *Employment and Immigration Canada Newsletter* Vol. 1, No. 16 (29 November 1979).

2. Catherine Dunphy, "Vietnam Refugees Now Part of Nation's Culture, Commerce," *Toronto Star* (9 March 1989), p. M8.
3. Penny Van Esterik and John Van Esterik, "Indochinese Refugees in Toronto," in *Ten Years Later: Indochinese Communities in Canada*, edited by Louis-Jacques Dorais, Kwok Bun Chan, and Doreen M. Indra (Montreal, 1988), p.119.
4. *The Vietnamese Community in Toronto*, Ethnocultural and Health Profiles of Communities in Toronto, No. 1 (Toronto, 1991).
5. Statistics Canada, *Census Canada '91*, No. 93-316 (Ottawa, 1991).
6. Ibid., data population by ethnicity.
7. Van Esterik, ibid.
8. Information gathered through informal interviews and observations in various neighbourhoods.
9. *The Vietnamese Community in Toronto*, ibid.
10. Lechi Oggeri, trans., "The Unique Characteristics of the Vietnamese Culture That Affect the Process of Adjustment of Vietnamese Refugees to American Culture." A PhD thesis submitted to the Department of Adult and Community College Education, North Carolina State University, Raleigh, NC, 1979.
11. Pierre Do Dinh, *Confucius et l' humanism chinois* (Paris, 1958), p. 128.
12. Arthur F. Wright, ed., *Confucianism and Chinese Civilization* (New York, 1964) pp. 1-15.
13. Maurice Percheron, *Le bouddha et le bouddhism* (Paris, 1956), p. 63.
14. *The Vietnamese Community in Toronto*, ibid.
15. Le Thanh Khoi, *Le Vietnam: Histoire et civilizatione* (Paris, 1955), p. 355.
16. Kenneth S. Latourette, *The Chinese, Their History and Culture* (New York, 1964), p. 549.
17. *Edmonton Magazine* Vol. 10, No. 3 (July 1988), pp. 53-54.
18. David Bai as cited in Lechi Oggeri, ibid.

Sri Lankan Tamils

The Segaran Family

Sujata Ramachandran

The riots that erupted in Colombo, Sri Lanka, in 1983 were the beginning of the end of life as the Segaran family had known it. By that time, deteriorating employment prospects for Tamils had already forced Siva Segaran to look for work outside Sri Lanka. Siva hailed originally from Jaffna, the traditional homeland of the Tamils in Sri Lanka. At the time of the riots, he was working abroad in Qatar, as a storekeeper for a hardware company in the small town of Doha.

During the riots, the Segaran house was razed to the ground and their possessions were looted. Vaseeharan, their only son who was seven years old at the time, went missing for several days. After Indira found her son, she fled with him, her two young daughters, and her elderly father on a perilous journey to the refugee camps in northern Sri Lanka. The camps proved to be no safer than Colombo.

Siva returned as quickly as he could to Sri Lanka and relocated the family to Jaffna. There, the new home they were building was destroyed even before it was finished. With the ethnic conflict escalating, Siva and Indira realized that they would have to leave Sri Lanka to survive.

A relative in Montreal urged Siva to consider Canada as a country of first asylum. At that time, Canada made special provision under a newly established program specifically for Sri Lankans who were affected by the events in Colombo. Canada also offered the possibility of full citizenship to these same newcomers. To reach Canada, however, would require a long and covert journey through Germany, France, and Italy.

In late 1984, Siva flew with five other Tamil men from Colombo to East Berlin, where they were admitted across the Berlin Wall to West Berlin on only a one-week visa. They took a train to the West German/French border where they stayed with other Tamil contacts. A German driver was bribed to drive them into France. Six Tamil men squeezed into a tiny two-wheel 'pet carrier' hitched to the back of the German driver's car. It was a six-hour drive in cold November. They stayed a week in Paris.

Without proper visas, Siva and his associates could not enter Italy where his brothers lived. Finally, they bribed the conductor of a train to put them in a rarely checked VIP compartment. They crossed the border undetected and stayed with relatives for two months just outside Rome in the town of Magliana.

At the time, there was much media coverage in Europe of Tamil refugees travelling with false passports. Siva stayed in Magliana until the coverage died down and he felt it was safe to fly (under an assumed identity) from Rome to Montreal. Once in Montreal, he declared his real name and nationality, and successfully sought refugee status. When Indira learned that Siva had reached Canada, she and the children moved to Madras, India, where they stayed from July 1985 to January 1988. The children attended school there until they could join their father in Canada.

Siva moved from Montreal to join the burgeoning Tamil community in Toronto. In 1988, he sponsored his family to join him and later his father-in-law, S.N. Rajah, who continues to live with them today. The Segarans keep in close contact with their extended family. Indira sponsored her maternal aunt a few years ago, and the family was helped by numerous relatives in the process of resettlement.

Most of the Segarans' friends and acquaintances belong to the Tamil community. Both Siva and Indira have worked in non-Sri Lankan environments, but express great satisfaction in serving their own community. Today, Siva Segaran is a settlement worker at the Tamil Eelam Society of Canada. His job includes helping refugees with resettlement, language instruction, skill training, and job placement in Ontario. Indira works, on contract, as an interpreter with the Immigration and Refugee Review Board. The eldest daughter, Mirunalini, is an eighteen-year-old undergraduate student at the University of Toronto, while seventeen-year-old Vaseeharan and ten-year-old Ketharini study in public schools near their home. At the time of this interview, the family was preparing to move to a condominium apartment in Scarborough.

The Segarans are well educated and proficient in English, which helped them to adapt to life in Canada. They also maintain traditional Tamil norms and values. The children are always reminded of their heritage, and there is an emphasis on Tamil religion and language. The Segarans appreciate their new freedoms, and the fact that, as Siva notes, "Canada encourages people to practise their own religion and culture."

The Segaran Family Speaks

Interviewed by Sujata Ramachandran

S *N. Rajah* I am eighty years old. I have been in Canada for four years. I came as a landed immigrant, and I stayed with my eldest daughter. My wife is dead, but I have another daughter and a son.

I was a lawyer. Then I became a Crown attorney. I was there for some time. Then I was in the legal department. Then I was seconded to the elections department. Then I was deputy commissioner, and then I was acting commissioner of elections for some time, so they confirmed my position in the government. I retired at the age of fifty-five and started practising again as a lawyer.

I was born in Jaffna, but most of my life was spent in Colombo, except for a few years. I went to university on a scholarship, and I got a first class in maths. I joined the law college and came out as a lawyer.

I am quite satisfied with Canada, except for the cold in the winter. Otherwise I am happy. People are very polite and helpful, especially to elders. I haven't experienced any racism. There is no racism. When it comes to the question of a job, you are basically a Canadian. There is no discrimination.

My eldest daughter is here, and we are trying to get my younger daughter to Canada. If she also comes, there is no point in my returning, except on a holiday for one month to see my old friends and family relations. I like to be where I am.

I own a lot of property in Jaffna. My properties are written to my children. In our family there is a lot of property, but most of it has been abandoned. There are three houses in a very large compound, but there is nobody to live in them.

We were in Colombo when the riots took place in July 1983. My daughters were living with me in a house that I had lived in for twenty years. We had to leave the house because we feared the riots. Part of the house was burnt. From there, we went to the refugee camp in Colombo, and were sent to Jaffna ten days later. My grandson was missing for three days. He had gone to school at seven o'clock in the morning. At that time we heard some commotion here and there, but we were not sure if things would get worse. By ten o'clock, everything flared up so that people were running and hiding here and there. We had to go.

My daughter was worried about her son, so I said that I would go to the school and bring him. And they waited. Then they said they would go to my niece's place. My niece sent a van to pick them up. I thought my grandson might vanish from the school. I couldn't find him by the time I arrived there. They said somebody took him, but they weren't sure who it was. Then I came back to my nephew's place.

The van came as expected. They put all of our things inside the van and proceeded to go to my nephew's place. Then half way through, they couldn't go on because the mob on the main roads were trying to assault people, asking people to get down, burning cars and all, so the driver of the van was really afraid. He said, "Ladies, you better get down. You should go to the nursing home. You will be safe there. You can bring the rest of the things later."

For three hours, they were in the nursing home. In the evening when things calmed down, they walked to my nephew's place, which is about three or four miles from the nursing home, so they walked. I was trying to find out where they went—whether they went to my nephew's place or to my brother-in-law's place. That night I took refuge at a friend's house. The curfew was on, so for three days we weren't allowed to go out. By the end of the third day, I went to the refugee camp, but they weren't there. Then I rushed to my nephew's place and they were all there. My eldest daughter was shocked to see me. They had thought Vasee

16. Ketharini Segaran and her grandfather, S. N. Rajah, Toronto, 1993 (Photo: Vincenzo Pietropaolo)

was with me. I told my daughter not to worry. Some Sinhalese people told me that they had seen my grandson. He has also gone to the refugee camp. I thought I'd take the bus and go there.

Before I got into the camp, somebody who knew me told me that my grandson was at the camp. My son, his wife, and children were there. My son was assaulted–he had a head injury. I did not know what to do. Fortunately, we saw the man who drove my grandson to school in a van every day. He asked us to get into the van and took us to my niece's place. Twice the mob tried to stop us. The Sinhalese people were killing Tamil people, burning them alive.

We heard about this and were horrified. The mob stopped us several times, but somehow we reached Wellawatta. Then all of us left for the refugee camp so we would be sent to Jaffna. Except for meals at my relatives' house, we stayed in the camp. Then we went to Jaffna by ship, staying there from 1984 to 1988. My son-in-law, Siva, came back from Doha. He could not stay permanently in Doha. He soon left for Canada in 1985. He didn't tell me why he wanted to go to Canada, but he wanted a safe place to live. It was not safe in Sri Lanka any more.

I was a Crown lawyer and had a difficult time. I had to defend the government on one side and the LTTE (Liberation Tigers of Tamil Eelam) on the other. I was their attorney several times. Some people warned me not to help the other group; I told them that I was doing it on humanitarian grounds. When the Indian peacekeeping force arrived in Sri Lanka, I was invited for many meetings. The commander of that area came to my home several times. I had to ask him to stop coming because I feared for my life. There were many factions. If you helped one group, the other group got annoyed. When someone was arrested, I would gladly rescue them by saying that he is an innocent man, but then it became impossible to stay safely at home–I had to sleep elsewhere. Sometimes at night if I heard a noise, I felt nervous and worried. Later, we went to India and stayed there for three years. Then later, my son-in-law sponsored us to Canada. With regard to adaptation, it depends on the community. We want to maintain our culture and it is welcomed by the Canadian government.

Siva Segaran My name is Siva Segaran. I am fifty-one years old. I have been working as a settlement worker at the Tamil Eelam Society of Canada for the last two and a half years. I came to Canada in January 1985. In Sri Lanka, I worked at the National Paper Corporation as a staff assistant in the accounts department and supplies department. I was in the insurance section. I was also a translator for three years. With my degree, I was able to manage all the sections successfully.

I lived in Valaichchenai in the Eastern Province of Sri Lanka for about three years, and the rest of the time I was living in Colombo. My father died in 1984. My mother, two sisters, and a brother are living in Jaffna.

In 1983, I felt that the Sri Lankan situation was not that good. I needed to work and had a chance to go to Doha, Qatar. Through a friend of mine, I got a job as a storekeeper in a hardware company there. I worked there for about one and a half years.

When I was in Doha, the violence in Sri Lanka took place in July 1983. In August 1983, I got word from my family that my seven-year-old son was missing for about three days, having never returned home from school. That worried me a lot, so I decided to go back to Sri Lanka. While I was waiting for an opportunity to tell the owner of the firm where I was working in Doha, my father died. I went back to Sri Lanka. I lived with my family in Jaffna until November. In the meantime, we started building a house also. Before I left Doha, the company owner was so happy with me that he secured a six-month visa for me. I told him what had happened and that I might have to stay for two or three months. He gave me a return ticket also.

Meanwhile, a relative of mine in Canada wrote to me and urged me not to go back to Doha. There were a lot of Tamil people going to Canada, he said. He told me that I could educate my children in English-language schools. It was the best time for anybody to go, so I thought I would try, and if I failed, I had the visa and I could always go back to Doha. I decided to come to Canada.

At that time, the East Berlin border was open to everyone. Sri Lankans needed entry visas. So we–myself, my brother, and another four of us–all started from Colombo. We purchased our tickets and we did not contact any agents because it was not necessary for us. We went to East Berlin and crossed the border. They faked the visas, I suppose, and allowed us to enter West Berlin. I had a relative living in West Berlin at that time. He said that he would wait at the railway station at West Berlin. He was there and took us to his house. We stayed one night with him. From there, he helped us the next day to go to West Germany. In the train when we were travelling, some ticket inspectors or immigration officials checked us and granted us two-day visas. We told them that we were going to France. We went to the West German border and waited there. One German was involved in taking people to France. At that time, it was very hard to go to France from West Germany, so he arranged a vehicle with a small pet-carrier connected to the vehicle. About six of us hid in that. He only cautioned us not to make any noise at a place where he stopped his vehicle.

This German man left us in France. We hired a taxi in France and went to a hotel where we stayed for a week. When we were in Paris, a few people contacted us. They were selling Mauritius passports and Singapore passports. We knew at that time that Singapore passports were not in use in any of the countries, so we asked for the Mauritius passports. We paid a few hundred dollars for each passport, and then we contacted my brothers. Two of them were living in Italy at that time. They were working in a garage about 10 miles from Rome. They told us to come to Italy. Even travelling from France to Italy was difficult.

Another relative of mine was in France at that time. He was very fluent in French, and he contacted some of the train engine drivers who were operating from France to Italy. We bribed those engine drivers and we got into a special compartment that was not checked. We reached Rome, where my brothers were waiting to receive me and my cousins. We went to their house and stayed in Magliana for nearly two months and in the meantime, we made arrangements to come to Canada.

We went to the Canadian embassy in Rome and were told that a visa was not required for those who held Mauritius passports. My brothers contacted a man who affixed our photographs to the Mauritius passports. We purchased our tickets and came to Canada.

Until 1986, a lot of Sri Lankans were living in Montreal. It was a pleasure to live with them instead of living in another province. I lived in Quebec because we wanted to have some sort of life with the same people, so I came to Montreal first.

Unfortunately, it was winter when I arrived. When I first landed in Montreal, it was so cold that I thought I had made a mistake in coming to Canada. But, little by little, I got used to it. I came in January 1985.

I had a lot of friends in Montreal. We used to visit one house or another, and sometimes they used to visit our place. I lived there for one and a half months and I was really enjoying it, but I moved to Toronto because of the employment problem. It was very hard to get a job those days in Montreal, especially for a refugee.

In Montreal I found it a little difficult because some people spoke to me in French even if I was talking to them in English. So I was a little cut off, alienated. But when I moved to Toronto, everybody (or the majority of people) spoke English. It was easier for me to find a job also. Sometimes I worked two jobs.

In Toronto I lived with my cousin who had wanted me to come to Canada. I lived with him for about two months. Later when we got accustomed to Toronto, we moved to an apartment on Jameson Avenue and lived there for one month.

It was easy to get jobs in restaurants in those days. I worked in a restaurant for about six months. Then I had a part-time job in a bakery and the bakery people said, "We like you. Why don't you come and work for us full-time?" I said I needed a lot of money now because I had to look after my family in Sri Lanka, but if they gave me good pay, then I would consider working for them. Then they told me they would give me a good salary and I started working there.

When I was in Toronto, I found that many Sri Lankans were misunderstood by most of the people because most of them were not fluent in English. So wherever they went, they could not explain what they wanted. When people were on welfare, they could not afford paying lawyers and other people to handle immigration matters. When I came, I stayed with my friends here. Little by little, people came to know about me and for small things like welfare, immigration matters, interpretation, and translation, they wanted me to accompany them.

I went with them and later on, other people came to know that I would oblige them if they asked me for help. Then that created a sort of friendship and people started respecting me because I was not accepting any money from anybody, that gave me an incentive to help more and more. When I started working, I helped people in my free time. I even went up to Ottawa to help them.

When the position of settlement worker for the Tamil Eelam Society of Canada was advertised, I applied and they asked about immigration matters, welfare matters, and where people can get help when they come to Canada for the first time. I was able to answer those questions simply because I had done those jobs earlier. They selected me and now I am still working in the same field. I am content because this is a job I know.

We do all types of work, especially immigration work. Our people need help in immigration matters. Most people who come to Canada are not aware of immigration matters. Most of them don't speak good English, or they don't know enough English to fill out those forms, or to understand the new immigration policy and welfare matters. These are the kinds of things they need help with the most. And since I had some experience when I was working in other places, I was of much help to them.

I write in newspapers about new rules and regulations about immigration or any laws amended with regard to common matters. Little by little, more people started coming in until there were the large numbers we get today. That shows that our organization is becoming popular, and people now learn more and more about our services. We have pamphlets describing what services we have. Many of the people who are newcomers know about us and they are coming to us for help.

There are other organizations asking for our services, and we are sending pamphlets. So when anybody who does not know about our society goes to other societies, they direct them here.

When I first came here, there was not more than 5,000 Tamils. Today our population is about 40,000 in Toronto alone. And in those days, there were more Tamils living in Montreal than in Toronto. Very few people came here. Now everybody thinks that Toronto is the best place to live. From about 1986 to 1992, it was very easy to find jobs. Most of the people needed some financial stability and most of them were working two jobs. Toronto was the best place for that, and that is why most people like living here. Now because of the recession, most people are laid off and jobless. Everybody expects that it might improve.

It was very hard for us to get our grocery items in those days. I remember that in 1985, there was only one Indian shop at Bloor Street and Lansdowne Avenue. Almost all of us used to go there to purchase curry leaves, chili powder, and other items that we used. Sometimes we were disappointed when there were no fresh curry leaves and we bought some dry leaves instead.

Today, there are more than 100 Tamil shops in the Toronto area. It is not a problem to purchase all those things now. Whatever things we used to get in Sir Lanka, we are able to get them here now. Recently the Tamil shops have even started selling fresh jackfruit directly imported from Sri Lanka. Now there is a lot of competition between business people to give the cheapest price. In those days, there was one price in almost all of the shops because things were scarce. Now things are available in plenty and there is a lot of competition, so we are able to purchase those things for half the price.

As far as I'm concerned, we are living the same life we led in Sri Lanka because there is no restriction in practising our culture or speaking our own language. Most of the people are mingling with other Tamils, and therefore we are leading the same type of life here.

As long as I am in the Tamil Eelam Society, I would have to be more of a Sri Lankan than a Canadian. And Canada encourages people to practise their own religion and culture here. There is a multicultural ministry, and they give funds to different communities to maintain whatever they had in their own country. So when they encourage it, naturally we should make the best use of it.

The Canadian government is trying to eradicate racism in this country. They are conducting seminars and spending a lot of money to eradicate racism, but in my work experience, I have observed racism frequently. The only advantage is that if you can prove it, they will be charged. You can even fight it in a court of law. This is a free country. You have every right to fight it out in the courts. That is a thing to be praised.

On the whole, I am happy that I brought my children to a good country where I can give them the best education. My two eldest children came here when they were about twelve and thirteen years of age, so they remember the life they lived in Sri Lanka and India, but I can see a little difference in the youngest one.

We attend almost all cultural activities and mix with the Tamil community regularly. Whenever we go to our relatives' house, we take our children, so they know what we like. They never displease us. They are obedient and they like the way of life we live. The youngest one would like to speak in English all the time because she can express herself better in English than in

17. Ketharini Segaran at her traditional Tamil coming-of-age ceremony in Toronto, 1993 (Photo: Vincenzo Pietropaolo)

Tamil. We always speak to our friends in Tamil. My children have no problem understanding.

When she left Sri Lanka, the youngest one was about two years old. She doesn't know much about our relatives. When we went back to Sri Lanka last year, I think it was the first time she saw my mother and other people. She left early so she couldn't remember most of her relations. But now she is old enough to remember them, so she really enjoys it. In fact, they wanted us to stay for several days. They all had a nice time with their cousins,

18. Siva and Indira Segaran with Ketharini the day of her coming-of-age ceremony in Toronto, 1993 (Photo: Vincenzo Pietropaolo)

my wife's sister's sons. We had a happy time there. Because my youngest daughter spent most of her life in Canada, returning to Sri Lanka was a very strange experience for her, but when she saw her cousins whom she hadn't seen for about five or six years, she behaved just like everybody else.

Even if the political situation gets better in Sri Lanka, I wouldn't go back immediately. My eldest daughter is in university and my son will also be going next year. I just can't spoil their lives or their future plans. They have to finish their studies first, so I have to think about migrating to Sri Lanka or anywhere else at a later date.

I would like to go back to Sri Lanka or India after I am sixty-five. For an old man, Canada is not the place to live. The weather is not suitable for old people. You can walk freely and safely in tropical countries, but not in Canada.

All my relatives are in Sri Lanka except for one brother living in Canada and two brothers living in Switzerland. When I move back to Sri Lanka, my children will have to decide whether to live with us or stay in Canada. I would not mind if they stayed in Canada as long as they maintain their culture and they don't forget the way of life Tamils lead in Sri Lanka. Deciding who to marry is a thing we have to decide later on. Even if it is my children's choice, if we like the people they choose, it is okay, but we would not like them to marry outside the community.

Canada is a good country. In Sri Lanka, we don't enjoy the language rights we enjoy in Canada. Here people have a good understanding. So, for anybody who wants to come and who wants advice from me about migrating to Canada, I always say it is good in Canada.

Meera Segaran My name is Meera, and I am eighteen years old. I was eight when the riots took place. On that day, the principal called and said don't come to school, so I didn't go. My brother had already gone to school. We left with my mother in the van. It was all fire and fights, and since there was no place in the front of the van, they put me in the back. And I saw everything. I closed my eyes, I was scared.

Then we went to a hospital. One of the nurses put us in the storeroom–me, my mom, my ten-month-old sister, my aunt, and her two kids. We were all there, and we heard all these noises of people killing each other. It was a hospital, but the armed forces came in and they were killing people. Then one of them tried to come into the storeroom, but one of the hospital staff said there was nothing in there. After they left, we walked to our cousin's house. There was glass everywhere, and the ground was so hot and everything. We were in a rush and we didn't have our shoes on, so we had to walk in those places. It was scary. My mom was crying all the time and my brother was lost. I didn't know much, I was only eight years old, but my mom was crying, so I basically cried with her.

We went to the refugee camp. It was like a big hall, no rooms or anything. People sleep in there and they supply you with food. You have to stand in line and get it. It was a safe place and there was no trouble in the camps. It was quiet. We just left everything. The driver said he would come back in three days. After three days, he came back. He said that people had burned the van that he took, but he escaped because he was a Sinhalese.

My mom's sister was there too. If we were going to go back to Jaffna, we had to stay in the camp and register, otherwise they won't let you go back. So what we did was stay with our aunt, and then at night, we would go to the camp, stay there, register our names, and then come back in the morning, take a wash, and then go back to the camp again.

My aunt's house was in a Sinhalese area and there were one or two Tamil families, so the army avoided that place, so it was much safer. All their kids know how to speak Sinhalese, and there were mostly Sinhalese families. One of my aunt's friends was protecting us, so it was not that bad.

I remember going to Jaffna in a ship and they put us on the deck. There were a lot of people on the ship–about 200 to 400

19. Mirunalini, Ketharini and Vaseeharan Segaran attended school in Madras, India in 1985 while they waited to come to Canada (Photo: courtesy of the Segaran family)

people. The ship was big. My grandfather got sick. They put hi
m in a room. We slept on the deck. They gave us mattresses and
everything. The trip took about three days. Some lady was sup-
plying food for the ship until it reached Jaffna. It was basically
bread, like sandwiches. We didn't have any other food. There
were about four or five bathrooms for 400 people. We didn't
actually see any fighting or bombing, but we could hear it. I remember the sound.

We lived with my mom's family in Jaffna. We arrived in
Jaffna in 1983 and left in 1985. Then we went to Madras for
three years.

My father came back in 1984 from Qatar, at the beginning of
the year and left towards the end. I went to school in India for
three years. I knew the place. Then my father went to Canada and
sponsored us in March 1988. I was thirteen when I arrived.

After we had settled in Toronto, I went to school for the last
three months of the school year. I had one of my Sri Lankan
friends, but she didn't understand English, so she went to ESL
classes.

Last year we went back to Colombo, Sri Lanka. I thought the
buildings would be burned down and there would be rioting, but
it was calm. There were no buildings that were burned down or
anything. They were rebuilt after the 1983 riots. And it was advanced. I didn't expect them to know about computers and they
have computer classes.

Here we attend almost all of the Tamil cultural programs, so
I have not lost my culture. At the same time, I have learned about
the Canadian culture, too, so I can see the difference between
them and choose the best without going against my culture. So I
didn't find much of a difficulty.

Vaseeharan Segaran My name is Vaseeharan and I am seventeen
years old. I have lived in Canada almost five years. We arrived
on 16 March 1988. I am going to high school. I am doing my
OAC courses right now.

Canada is okay. You don't have so much violence here like back in Sri Lanka, and here the people are very nice and kind. They are not so racist or anything like that.

I'm not saying that there isn't any racism, but so far I have not experienced any. There are racist jokes that I have heard, but people don't call me names or stuff like that.

Parkdale is the most multicultural school in Toronto. Most of the students are non-white. I'm going to university next September. I think I want to go into arts and science.

The weather here is very different. Sri Lanka is a tropical country and here when we came, it was almost spring, but it was still cold. Back in Sri Lanka I have my cousins and everyone is there–most of my relatives. And I think it is better there. Here it is always rushing–you go out of the house in the morning and you come back at night, and you don't have time to do anything else.

But back in Sri Lanka, school closes early and you could come back and do whatever you want. And you have more free time there. I think school ended there around one o'clock. Here it is three o'clock, but I still have to go to the library and do my homework or projects if I have any.

We have a lot of relatives here. Whenever we have free time, we see them, mostly on the weekends. In our neighbourhood in Sri Lanka, all the families lived close together, so we didn't have to go to the relatives' house. We all lived so close that we didn't have to visit any more.

The riots started in Sri Lanka, and we didn't know. We were at home. I had gone to school in a van. After I left, the principal phoned and said don't come to school. Don't leave the house. But it was too late, I had already left. When I got to school, only a few people were there. So the school sent us home in the school bus. On the way back, there were fires and people dead on the street. I was eight years old. I went home and knocked on the door and no one was home. Our neighbour was at home and said my parents will be back to pick me up.

I was staying at the neighbour's house when some thugs broke in. They ran one way and I ran the other way. Afterwards, they went into our house. I saw them break into our house, break all the furniture, and burn the house. Then I went to one of my grandfather's friends. He was still at home and I stayed at his house. Then the thugs came. My neighbour told the thugs that there were no Tamils in his house. There was a Salvation Army close by. All the Tamil people were there and we had protection and everything. After two or three days, some of the neighbours and I were put into a refugee camp. I stayed there and I found my aunt and two cousins there. We were preparing to go north where my other relatives were. On my third day in the refugee camp, my grandfather came looking for me and he found me, and that's how I got home.

We left for India in 1985, I think July or August. One of my relatives left two or three months before us and they found a place to live there and we went after that. We already had relatives living there for two or three years, so we had some people to show us around.

We went to a relative's house–me, my grandfather, and my three cousins. We were playing there and a tank blew up. It exploded near our house. We were trapped in there and there was fighting going on around the house. We had to stay there until the next morning. When everything calmed down, we went back to our own house. That is the closest I have been to a fight–a battle.

When we went back to Sri Lanka, it was the same as I re-membered it. We had to go to the Canadian High Commission and sign a register to say that we are in Sri Lanka. If there were no troubles, I'd like to go back to Sri Lanka. My parents would like to go back. They don't like Canada's weather. Most of our relatives are in Sri Lanka. We don't have much time to talk to our relatives here, and we don't have much free time or anything like that. It would be a better life in Sri Lanka, if there were no troubles.

Indira Segaran My name is Indira Segaran. I am forty-five years old. I have three children, Meera, Vasee, and Ketha. I am a Sri Lankan Tamil. I was born in Colombo, but my native place is Jaffna. I came to Canada in 1988.

I work at the Immigration and Refugee Board as an interpreter. I used to work for school communities, too. I started working in 1990. Before that I worked for a firm called Roblan Distributors. At the same time, I was working for the school community board. I am a member of the heritage study class at Queen Victoria Public School and an executive member of the Parent-Teacher's Association at Fern Public School. In the evenings, sometimes I act as an interpreter in parent-teacher interviews.

I was an inventory clerk at Roblan Distributors. Later, after one year, I was promoted to an accounts payable clerk. Then in May 1990, I had to undergo surgery and after that I quit that job. I was without work for some time and at home for a few months. I like my present job better than the other job. I get the chance to work with my own people, my own community, so I really like it.

Back home, I was a high school teacher for thirteen years in Colombo Ladies College. I remember it was 25 July 1983 when the riots took place. We were having the second term exams and I was in charge of the exams for the whole school. So in the morning, I was getting ready to go to school to distribute the papers for the teachers and students and all that, and I had to be on time to get all the things prepared. I got a call from the principal of the school and she told me that she had heard of a few incidents of rioting and advised that it was not safe to leave for school that day. She said, "Mrs Siva Segaran, do not come to school today. We cannot ask the students not to come to school because it is a government school and we cannot do that. But you don't come. Let the students come, we can send them home."

My eldest daughter was studying in the same school where I was teaching. My youngest daughter was then six months old and my son was studying at St Thomas College. It is a bit far away from our place, so he used to go to school by a van that came to collect him around seven a.m. He had left for school before I received the call from my principal. In addition, my husband was working in Doha in the Middle East. At my house, my father and my only sister were also staying with me. She is also married and has two kids. Her husband was also working in the Middle East at the same time.

Then around ten o'clock we got news that they were planning to attack that area–the riots were spreading to the area. I did not know what to do. So I rang up my cousin in Bamblapettiya, which is about 6 miles from the place where we were staying. She told me that she would send a van for all of us and take us to her place. In the meantime, my father said that he would go and collect my son from school and would join us later in Bamblapettiya.

The van and the driver soon arrived and we packed a few things like jewellery, cash, valuables, and our passports. We all got into the van, including me, my two daughters, my sister, her two kids, and two servant girls I had. On the way, we were informed that we could not pass the main street because of looting and that shots were being fired from either side. I told the driver to take us to the nearest post office because I knew the postmaster there–he was a good friend of ours. He was Sinhalese. But the moment we reached the post office, the postmaster told me, "Mrs Segaran, it is very dangerous to keep you all here. You should try and go to Wellawatha, which is a Tamil area. You can be safe there." He did not want to accommodate us. He was afraid of the employees in the post office because they were all Sinhalese. He was worried that they might harm us or something.

Actually, the driver of the van was also Sinhalese. I had no choice but to tell the driver to take us to Bamblapettiya. There was no other option. So he took us by the smaller lanes, avoiding the main streets, which were being attacked by the mobs. Finally, we reached Wellawatha, but we could not pass through. The mob was there with daggers, swords, and other weapons. I was so scared. I told the driver to take us to the Wellawatha police station. We went into the police station. When we pulled the van into the police station, the constable there started scolding us and using obscene language. He said, "Oh, you people, you Tamils–don't come here because we are not going to protect you. Go away and get away from this place."

So we did not have any choice but to leave for the main streets again. Then the driver spoke to me in Sinhalese. He said that he could not take us any further, that he would either drop us there on the main road or leave us somewhere nearby, so I told him to take us to the nearby hospital/private nursing home. I thought that the hospital would be safe and that we would not be attacked there.

At the hospital we met a labourer and he asked us to leave all our things and go with him. And luckily, I had taken my daughter's milk bottle because she was only six months old. I took the children, my sister, and her sons and went inside the hospital. I was carrying the baby and the two servant girls were also with me. This labourer took us inside the storeroom. He said, "Go stay there and be silent. Don't make any noise."

When I went inside the room, I was horrified to see a man–an Indian man who was bleeding. He was bleeding profusely and he started crying loudly when he saw me. He was just a young man. I nearly fainted after seeing his wounds. This man was working in a Sinhalese restaurant and the mob attacked him and cut him on the neck. I told the young man to be silent or all of us would be discovered and be in trouble.

We forgot all about our valuables in the van–jewellery, money, everything, but the labourer brought our handbag and said the driver was reluctant to keep the van outside because it was not safe. He was taking the van to the house and promised to come and bring the other things. He was afraid that he would be discovered by the mobs. We did not mind this–we were not concerned about other things as long as we were safe. We had forgotten about our valuables, but the labourer rescued those for us.

We could see and hear the mobs attacking the nursing home from all sides. They were throwing bottles and all. It was only later that we were told the mobs came looking for some Tamil doctors who worked in the nursing home. They were attacking the Tamil patients there. We stayed in the storeroom for more than half an hour. The mob also came to check the storeroom and we heard someone telling them from outside that they do not keep any patients in that room and that it is only a storeroom. Fortunately they decided not to see the room after all and went away.

After about one or two hours, the labourer returned and said that he did not mind keeping us in the nursing home because we would be safe, but his life would be in danger if the other Sinhalese employees at the nursing home discovered that he was sheltering some Tamils. He added that the others would kill him. Most of the employees at that place were Sinhalese. They did not want to keep us or protect us. He told us that he would take us to my cousin's place in Bamblapettiya if I wanted. I agreed to leave for my cousin's place. I was also very worried about my father and son. I had lost contact with them and I did not even know whether they were safe or not.

We finally went to my cousin's place. I told my cousin's husband what had happened. I told him that I must immediately go and look for my son, but he said, "You cannot travel now because it is too dangerous. We can ask one of the Sinhalese people to help in this situation. He is a retired officer and may be able to help us." When this officer came home, I told him all the details, he asked me to write a letter to the principal, authorizing him to bring my son. This person is a stranger and my son would not know him. He was my cousin's neighbour.

Immediately I wrote a letter to the principal and I also wrote a letter to my son saying, "Vasee, this man is so and so. You better come with him at once. It is safe and we are at this place. You can come and join us." This man took the letter and later came and told us that the principal had told him that my son had already left with the van driver. Three days' mental agony for me.

There was a curfew. I could not go out anywhere. I was all alone with small children. And I could not leave them anywhere. I had no support, you know. And after three days when they lifted the curfew, my father came looking for us at my cousin's place. He said that he could not locate my son because he could not reach the school. He was travelling in a bus that was attacked by the mob. They were harassing all the Tamils on the bus. Somehow my father managed to escape and spent some time at a friend's place. I said, "Oh my God! I have lost my son forever." My father then said that he would go to the place where we lived and find out what happened to my son.

When he went there, he was told by a neighbour that he had seen Vaseeharan during the riots. Apparently, the van driver had dropped him outside the house and he had been roaming the streets looking for us. He could not find us anywhere. Finally, there was a reverend who lived near our house who kept him in the Salvation Army at night with the other Tamils. Later he was transferred to the camp at Ratmalana. My father went to the Ratmalana camp looking for him. There he not only found my son but also my brother with his family, including his wife and two children. My brother had a cut on his head and had broken his arm. They all took refuge there. After some time, my father brought my son home.

My son saw the riots. To tell you the truth, I have not spoken to him about it. I do not want him to think about it and worry about it. I have my son, that is more than enough. I should thank God for that.

We stayed at my cousin's place for a week or so and that was the time when I was able to contact Siva and tell him what happened. During the riots, the telephone lines that went to Tamil houses had been cut so that they could not communicate with the outside world. That was a tactic, so I was unable to contact Siva immediately after it happened. My father's brother was staying on the next street. He visited us and told us that we would be able to use his phone because it was working, so my sister and I went

20. Siva and Indira Segaran from the balcony of their new home in Scarborough, 1993 (Photo: Vincenzo Pietropaolo)

one morning and I was able to contact Siva. My husband and brother-in-law were both working at the same place in Doha, Qatar. We contacted both of them. They were very upset to hear what had happened. Even at that time, I did not tell Siva that our son was missing for three days. I did not wish to upset him.

At that time in Jaffna, they were giving funds to the people affected by the riots, so I was able to get some money and I started building a house. In the meantime, we lived in fear. I was renting out a small annex in Jaffna because my children were going to school there. We were sharing with another family. Sometimes in the morning the children would go to school, and at ten o'clock they would be sent home because there was some fighting.

Then Siva went to Canada and we moved to Madras, India. We liked it there in Madras. It was the same as Jaffna. I had been to India and I studied in Lucknow. It was a little expensive, and we had to rent out a flat and schooling was expensive. Siva was sending money from Canada.

I was not working. I did a course in computers there. I did my basic programming. I did a project for the housing board and a computer course. Then I learned typing. I was on a tourist visa, so I was not allowed to work there. Then Siva got his papers and sponsored us.

When I first came to Canada, I had some problems with my dresses and all. I didn't know that I would be able to wear a sari here all the time. In fact, at the first interview I went to, I wore a sari, and the counsellor advised me that this is Canada, you have to change a lot. Cut your hair, wear it short. I said I am not going to cut my hair. She was really insistent. Immediately after that, I got into an immigration office program. It was really good and three months later, after I was given job training, I was working at Roblan Distributors.

The Sri Lankan Tamil Community

Arul S. Aruliah

The Tamil community in Canada has a population size of about 73,000 in 1994[1], and an overwhelming majority–about 93 per cent–of them have come from Sri Lanka (or Eelam, as it is known in Tamil) in the last decade. Most originate from the Jaffna district in the Northern Province, and hence are known as Jaffna Tamils. They were admitted under some form of humanitarian and compassionate considerations as a result of the continuing communal conflict in that country. Other immigrants from Sri Lanka–Sinhalese, Malays, and Burghers–constitute about 10 per cent of the total Sri Lankan population of about 75,000 in Canada. A total of eighty landings were recorded in 1964 who declared themselves as citizens of Sri Lanka–or Ceylon, as it was known then. There were another 4,300 Sri Lankan immigrants landed–of which about 30 per cent were Tamils—in the next two decades, and the others arrived in the last decade.

Tamils constitute about one-fifth of the population of Sri Lanka (17.4 million in 1991), and India has a Tamil population of about 55 million in the south Indian state of Tamil Nadu. Tamil immigrants from India constitute about 6 per cent of the Canadian Tamil population, with less than 1 per cent from Malaysia, Singapore, Fiji, Mauritius, Trinidad, Guyana, and South Africa–descendants of the colonial migrants from India. Common cultural linkage notwithstanding, historically Jaffna Tamils have developed a distinct social tradition from that of Tamils of India. Today, the Sri Lankan Tamil community is often seen as synonymous with both the Sri Lankan community and the Tamil community in Canada.

Early Tamil migrants to Canada–just like other post-1967 migrants from developing nations admitted under the immigration points system—were mostly professionals and their families. They were scattered across the country in major cities, with the largest proportion living in Toronto and Montreal. Presently, nearly 90 per cent of Tamil Canadians live in the greater Toronto region–Ajax to Oakville to Richmond Hill–and this population represents a cross-section of the home country population. An estimated Tamil population of 5,000 lives in Montreal, with much smaller groups of Tamils living in other major cities, such as Ottawa, Winnipeg, Edmonton, and Vancouver.

As a young community in Canada, the Tamil community has very close connections with both its language and culture. The propagation of Tamil language is fairly assured among recent immigrants, whose family conversations, social gatherings, and cultural programs are conducted almost entirely in Tamil. However, a significant proportion of children who were either born in Canada or came as very young children can understand the language cursorily but do not speak it (again, a phenomenon evident among immigrant communities). As a result, a series of weekend heritage language classes have been organized within several municipal school boards. Students are learning Tamil as they would German, Spanish, or French in high school, and they obtain the appropriate credit for each grade level.

There is a significant emphasis on classical Tamil arts: *Carnatic* vocal and instrumental music and *Bharata Natyam* (the ancient dance form). The increased population has produced not only a greater demand for lessons of this type but also for a large number of qualified teachers, who have established various academies and schools. Almost every weekend, there are many programs held in school auditoriums in greater Toronto that are often a combination of classical, folk, and popular Tamil culture.

Tamil poetry and prose are being promulgated by Tamil-language newspapers, which print stories and poems composed by Canadian Tamils. The newspapers themselves are a reflection of the requirements of the burgeoning population. There are about six weekly newspapers and monthly publications available in Toronto. As well, a few Tamil books have been published. The advent of desktop publishing technology and the exponential growth rate of Tamil immigrants has produced almost a cottage industry in Tamil publication. The media impact, however, is not limited to print. Within the last five years, there has been an increased frequency of Tamil radio programs, and since 1994 there have been daily programs on the radio and one weekly television show on the commercial network and one on the community channel. Most programs are largely variety shows, consisting of news and information, dance and music items, plays and speeches.

An estimated 15–25 percent of the Canadian Tamil population are Christian, and the rest of the community follows the *Saivite* form of Hinduism–its philosophy traces its roots to the 5,000-year-old Indus Valley civilization. As Megan Mills has observed,[2] "Hinduism of this variety is noted for its open-minded style: the tradition encourages the individual to follow his or her own path to union with the divine .... Consequently, religious affiliation does not command any stronger "loyalty" than cultural affinity. A remarkable reflection of this non-dogmatic religious affiliation is demonstrated by the universal celebration of Christmas in Tamil homes, and a just-as-packed temple attendance for Gregorian New Year *pooja* as for the Tamil New Year that falls on 13–14 April. Only a few Tamil-speaking people of Islamic faith have immigrated to Canada.

Religious ceremonies are very common in traditional family homes. Three temples have been founded by the Tamil community in the greater Toronto area, and many of the festivals that are observed in Jaffna, Sri Lanka, are simultaneously observed in Canadian temples. The Hindu Temple Society of Canada, with significant participation from people of south Indian heritage (Tamil, Telugu, Kannada, and Malayalee), has built one of the largest Hindu temples in North America. It is located in

Richmond Hill, Ontario. In addition to temple ceremonies, weekly *bhajans* (meditation by singing devotional songs) are conducted by numerous local groups. A number of Christian churches, whose congregations are predominantly Tamil, have also been established. These Tamil churches provide spiritual leadership and function as counsellors for domestic and social issues.

There are several community organizations in Toronto that serve a variety of purposes. In many cases, specific organizations have been formed to address particular needs of the community. The Tamil Eelam Society of Canada, which was founded in 1976 by a small group of Eelam (Sri Lankan) Tamils as a social and cultural group, was transformed into a volunteer-based settlement agency in 1983. Since 1989, it has been supported by various government agencies for the delivery of settlement services.

The World Tamil Movement (WTM) promotes social and cultural values among Tamils in Canada and overseas through its network of volunteers. It also publishes a free, bi-weekly newspaper, *Ulaga Thamilar* ("World Tamils"), and produces a weekly radio program in Toronto. Founded in 1985, WTM pays particular attention to human rights violations in Sri Lanka.

Another organization, Senior Tamils Centre of Ontario (based in Don Mills), assists seniors with counselling and recreational activities. The Canada Ceylon Tamil Chamber of Commerce of Ontario assists the mercantile sector, and the Association of Sri Lankan Graduates of Canada provides referral assistance to professionals to upgrade their skills.

The sudden growth of the community from the late 1980s, has led to the formation of a large number of social groupings, most notably based on organizations of alumni of Jaffna schools. These organizations serve as close-knit affinity groups, and have been active in the rebuilding program of their war-damaged schools. Affordable housing has been one of the major sources of concern for the new immigrants, resulting in a relatively high degree of shared home-ownership. There is one co-operative home in Toronto and another is under construction in Mississauga.

The degree of individual interaction with the wider community at large has naturally been a function of that person's fluency in the English language (in Toronto where most have settled). Those who are young and sufficiently fluent in English have found jobs in commercial and industrial sectors. Many are working in the service sector. A large number of the new immigrants have gone into self-employment. A recently published directory, *Amidst Tamils '93*[3], lists nearly 400 pages of Tamil business advertisements providing every kind of service. There are many two-income households, and nearly 80 per cent of the population is under fifty years of age. Education is given an extraordinary amount of attention by parents who themselves are upgrading their skill level; and a number of students have secured places in the universities. Within the context of the multicultural mosaic in large Canadian cities, this young community–well studied general immigrants' settlement difficulties notwithstanding–has used its strong family-value systems to integrate remarkably well within a decade of their arrival in Canada.

Notes

1. See *Refuge*, Vol. 14, No. 4 (1994), for a detailed profile of the community. Figures quoted in this essay are drawn from "Accepted on Compassionate Grounds: An Admission Profile of Tamil Immigrants in Canada." For a detailed analysis of the communal conflict, please see the special issue of *Refuge*, Vol. 13, No. 3 (1993) on Sri Lanka. *Refuge* is published by the Centre for Refugee Studies at York University.
2. See ibid.
3. *Amidst Tamils '93* (Scarborough, Ont., 1993).

Somalis

21. Yusuf Abdi, statesman and activist in the democratic movement in Somalia, 1989. He perished while escaping with his three eldest children (Photo: courtesy of the Abdi family)

The Abdi Family

Edward Opoku-Dapaah and Elizabeth McLuhan

Following his violent abduction and imprisonment, Yusuf Abdi, the director of an international agency that supported the democratic movement in Somalia, realized that he and his family could no longer stay in their country's war-torn capital, Mogadishu. Yusuf arranged for his wife, Faduma, who was pregnant at the time, to leave with their two youngest children, one of whom is severely disabled with muscular dystrophy. They made their way from Kenya through the United States to Canada, where Faduma sought refugee status in December 1989. Meanwhile, Yusuf tried to escape by boat to Kenya with his two oldest daughters, Amina and Filsan, and his only son, Fahiye. The overloaded boat capsized. The children made it to shore only to see their father drown while helping others.

The seventeen-year-old Amina, in shock, wandered among the wreckage on the shore and talked to other survivors from their boat. While Amina watched her father and her aunt die, she still had her sister and her brother with her. She met those who had lost their entire family. Amina took heart and counted herself lucky. It fell to her, the oldest, to try to keep the three of them together and alive.

In Toronto, Faduma feared that all four had perished. It was only later that she learned the truth. The three children were sent to a Red Cross refugee camp and later moved covertly to a relative's home in Nairobi. And it was not until July 1991 that the mother and children were reunited.

Today they live in a high-rise apartment block in Etobicoke. Five children are in school with the youngest, Canadian-born

Warsan, still at home. Faduma, a well-educated woman who worked as an accountant in Somalia, is frustrated at her unemployed status. With several other Somalis, she is establishing a local community group in Etobicoke to help Somali families in a similar predicament.

Faduma Adbi was born in 1955 at Jalalagsi, located in the heartland of Somalia, 120 kilometres from the capital city of Mogadishu. After graduation from the Somali National University, she worked at the Ministry of Treasury and Finance. Later she volunteered her time to human rights groups and agencies that assisted the 400,000 Ethiopian refugees who fled to Somalia since the late 1970s. Her husband, Yusuf Abdi, was born in Erigavo in 1939. He studied in Yemen, Britain, and the former Soviet Union. He was a two-term member of Parliament and a university lecturer. He was fluent in seven languages and a respected statesman.

In 1986, civil war broke out in the northern part of Somalia between two rival factions–the Somalian National Movement and United Somalia Congress. The war raged on and spread. The conflict threatened life and stability, giving rise to mass condemnation and criticism of the current government. In an effort to clamp down on opposition and re-establish control, the governing military resorted to mass arrests, intimidation, abductions, and all forms of coercive tactics.

Yusuf Abdi belonged to an underground group, the Democratic Action League (DAL), a middle-class opposition group strongly opposed to the Siad Barre regime. In the midst of the clampdown on opposing elements, DAL members became targets of the dictatorial regime.

In 1989, when Yusuf Abdi was detained in prison, soldiers invaded the family home, terrorizing Faduma and the children. They ransacked the house. Faduma was forced to seek refuge in the countryside. Influential clan members in the army helped Yusuf to escape after two months. Soon afterwards, Yusuf Abdi made plans to remove the entire family from Somalia.

Reunification with her three oldest children in Canada could not mask the profound sense of loss that Faduma felt for her husband who died while escaping. Such grief is compounded by never having said good-bye to him, and never being able to have a proper funeral for the man who was a central figure in her life. For Faduma and all the children except the youngest, Warsan, Yusuf Abdi's absence continues to be a bitter fact of daily life.

Faduma waited in the refugee backlog for a year before completing the refugee admission process. Immigration authorities declared that even though Faduma fit the United Nations Convention refugee definition, Hibaq, her disabled child, was not medically admissible. This affected the entire family's chances of staying in Canada. It took a year to resolve the complications surrounding Faduma's immigration status, but this was only after the intervention of church groups and African community advocates.

Faduma received help from fellow Somalis when she arrived in Toronto. Her compatriots took her to the social services department where she applied for assistance. Nevertheless, Faduma continues to face numerous resettlement challenges. Since her arrival in 1989, she has been unable to enter a language-training program due to a lack of proximity to a training centre, the special requirements of her disabled child, and prohibitive baby-sitting costs. Also, limited proficiency in English has affected her present job prospects compared to her prior occupation and academic attainments.

Faduma's children were nineteen, seventeen, fourteen, eight, seven, and three at the time of this interview. They live in a three-bedroom apartment. Her efforts to get a handicap-accessible residence for her child have been unsuccessful. She found her present apartment through Metro Toronto Housing, but the neighbourhood is unsafe. The area is a hang-out for drug pedlars and addicts, and she and the children live in fear. Incidents of crime and attacks are rampant. The children have code-named the apartment "hell house."

Faduma considers Canada as a whole to be a safe haven, a place of abundant security from the persecution, intimidations, and famine that have afflicted the people of Somalia. Her mind is not at peace, however, because she and her children face dangers of a different kind on a daily basis. Memories of what she and her children have endured, the loss of her husband, compounded by the hardships associated with daily life in Toronto, give her no respite.

In October 1993, Faduma, Amina, Filsan, Fahiye, Hodan, and Hibaq received their landed immigrant papers.

The Abdi Family Speaks

Interviewed by Edward Opoku-Dapaah
and Elizabeth McLuhan

F aduma Abdi I met my husband, Yusuf Abdi, in 1973 and we were together until he died in 1991. I was studying at secondary school when I got married. I finished university in 1983. My degree is in economics. After that I worked for the Ministry of Treasury and Finance.

I had children and continued my education at the same time. Life in Somalia is much cheaper and easier than it is here in Canada. Here, it is very difficult to study and have children at the same time, but back home it is quite different.

In Somalia, there are other people to help care for the children because you have many relatives. Your mother-in-law, your mother, and your sisters live with you and take care of you. We live side by side, very close, and sometimes we have our housekeeper, our babysitter. They are affordable. So you can have your babysitter and housekeeper at the same time. Life goes on.

In Somalia, there is no law that says women cannot work after they get married, but it depends on the person. Some people are very rigid and believe that women should stay at home and take care of the children. Luckily my husband was progressive and he helped my education. He taught me sometimes. He was a very wonderful man.

I was about seventeen years old when I got married. Yusuf was a very special person. He was my best friend, he was my husband, and he was my teacher. Sometimes he was like my parent. So he was my life. We had been neighbours. I was very active in my community, even though I was very young, so that's how we met there. We were trying to help organize community

22. Faduma Abdi, 1993. Faduma, university-educated, was an accountant in Somalia. Now a single parent, she co-founded the Somali Community Centre of Etobicoke (Photo: Vincenzo Pietropaolo)

activities. He was one of the top community leaders in our area. We were socialists and at that time we didn't even have a party. Somalia was under the control of the military, so there were no political organizations in the country. It was prohibited. If we were found out, we would be in danger. We would die or maybe we would be in a jail for the rest of our lives. My husband was sometimes more aware than others of what was happening around us at that time. The other people were obedient or followers of the military dictatorship. My husband couldn't state his opinions publicly, but he was trying to mobilize secretly. He was working with the government and at the same time he was high commissioner in the NRC in UNHCR [United Nations High Commissioner for Refugees]. It was what they call the National Revenue Commissioner under UNHCR. He was also a member of Parliament and well known in Mogadishu, particularly among those who are progressive people.

I became involved in politics after I met my husband. My parents were not politically involved. I did not analyse anything before I met my husband, but I was open-minded. So when I met Yusuf, he tried to teach me the reality behind the myth. He tried to explain to me and some of my other friends what the military dictatorship really meant and what we needed. Everything was going from bad to worse and the government was dysfunctional. Yusuf was one of the few people who were trying to overthrow the existing government and mobilize an underground democratic movement, but it was not public yet. He was the president of the Democratic Action League.

We both recognized that things were getting worse. We knew that he would be in prison someday, so we decided to leave. I was pregnant at the time. My two youngest daughters and I left Somalia first. We came to Canada in 1989. Yusuf tried his best to stay in Somalia and continue the struggle. I got a visa from the United States embassy, then I went to the United States and stayed in Washington for four days. I crossed the border into Canada because my sister was in Toronto. I declared myself a refugee. It was Christmas time. It was a very wonderful day in my life. My sister Maka is younger than me. She's been here about four years. When she first came, she said, "Don't stay anywhere else. Canada is the best place besides our country. Please come to me. Canada is a very beautiful country, very good people." She came three months before me. When I was still back home, she called and said, "You know, it's time for you to leave before it's too late."

She encouraged me to come because she knew of the situation back home. She was an airline hostess and she goes to many regions. She sees what is going on over there. She knew more than anybody else because she has seen with her own eyes what's going on in another region. She said that Siad Barre will destroy Somalia, that I have to escape before I die. She got many threats from them because they said she was helping those people who were trying to escape.

Amina is my oldest daughter, Filsan is my second, Fahiye is my third and he's the only boy that I have in my family. Hodan is my fourth, Hibaq (the disabled one) is my fifth, and Warsan, the Canadian one, was born here. Warsan is not a refugee, she is a Canadian citizen. She is three years old now. The luckiest ones are my three youngest daughters because they did not see what was going on in Somalia. We left when Mogadishu was still calm. Now my nine-year-old girl, Hodan, has started school here in Canada. She speaks English fluently without any accent so you know she's more Canadian. Now she's in grade three. She will be in grade four this September. My handicapped child, Hibaq, will be in grade two this September, and Warsan is the only one with me at home. Amina will finish high school this coming year. Filsan is in grade ten and Fahiye will be in grade nine next year. Three of them are in high school and the others are in elementary.

Amina, Filsan, and Fahiye (the three oldest children) were with their father back home. They have seen with their own eyes what was going on in Somalia. They fled from Somalia to Kenya in order to join us. They were in a boat that sank. It was incredible, unbelievable.

23. Amina, Filsan, and Fahiye Abdi with a cousin in the compound of their home in Mogadishu, 1990 (Photo: courtesy of the Abdi family)

It is really a new life for me. Having all these children far away from the rest of my family, in a new country where you don't know what is good for you and what is bad is very difficult. In Somalia, marrying young, I didn't make my own decisions. It is a very big responsibility for me now, but, thank God, my children are very good children. My eldest daughter, Amina, is the second mother. She helps me a lot because she has a lot of experience already. She's nineteen, but she is much wiser than a nineteen-year-old child because of her experience. Even though it's been very hard, I discuss things before I make a decision with my children. I prepare them to make their own decisions and at the same time they help me. I was a friend of my father before I left my home. My father was my best friend. Besides my mum, I love my daddy more than my mum, and my husband was my best friend also. My experience is to be close to the parent or the person you share life with, so my children are my best friends now. I don't have very many problems. Even with the difficulties, I'm still one of the luckiest to have my children with me. They obey my orders and we make decisions together, we discuss everything together, we learn together, so we are very close.

Back home when I was in grade five to grade twelve, I studied English. After that, I learned Italian at university, but I forgot it because back home we were always speaking our language. I forgot English and now when I come here, I don't get a chance to go to school for even one day, but I am remembering it.

Now I learn English from my children and teach them at the same time. At first I taught them because I knew more than they did, but now they teach me because they know more than I do.

We are Muslims, we believe in the Islamic religion, and we practised it in our country. People from all over the world, every

24. The Abdi family in their Etobicoke home (left to right) Hodan, Hibaq, Filsan, Amina, Faduma, Fahiye and (centre) the youngest, Warsan, 1993 (Photo: Vincenzo Pietropaolo)

continent, every country maybe, come to Canada, so all the religions are here. We go to the mosque on Fridays instead of Sunday like the Christians. On Saturday and Sunday, there are certain religious classes, but sometimes it is difficult to get transportation. The nearest mosque is on Dundas. It's too far away, so sometimes it is difficult to go there. I'm Muslim, but I'm not a very religious person. We have our own clothes and our own culture. We like and are very proud to wear our traditional dresses in the summertime. Whether you are very religious or not, winter is your master because you have to wear what the other people are wearing. You have to wear the boots, the gloves, and what other people wear. But in the summertime, we are very comfortable wearing our dresses, our style. If you are married, you have to cover your hair. That's for religious purposes. We have different *sheekh* (religious leaders). Those are in the top ranks of the religion. In some circles, if you are a woman, whether you are married or not, you have to cover your body except for maybe your eyes, your face. Our tradition is the Somali tradition. We cover our hair and our body. We are all Muslim, but some wear short dresses the way that they like. They pray five times a day, but they wear whatever they like, and others have some restrictions, but it depends, just like Catholicism.

We pray five times a day. Sometimes we pray as a family, but it is not compulsory to do it together. Amina prays on her own and the others do so as well, but on the weekend, if we are all together, we pray together in the morning (*Subah*), at noon (*Duhur*), evening (*Asar*), (*Macrib*) and the final prayers (*Isha*). That's five prayers. We pray before sunrise, after two o'clock, at six, at nine, and at ten we pray the last one before we go to bed. If it is not possible for them to pray during the day, when they come home, they have a late prayer.

My children socialize with the people at school and maybe they make conversation, but we are different from Canadian girls

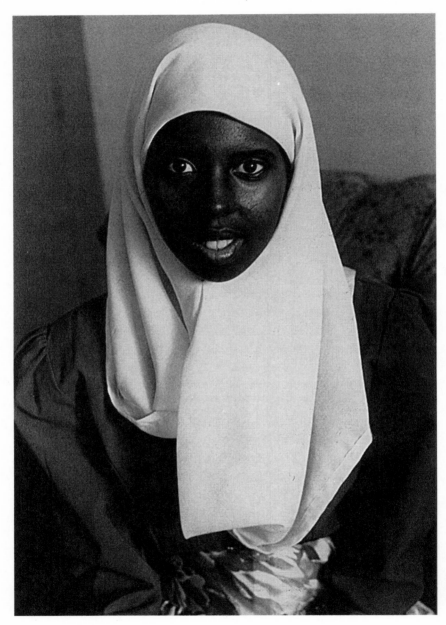

25. Filsan Abdi, Toronto, 1993 (Photo: Vincenzo Pietropaolo)

who want boyfriends. This is prohibited in our culture or our religion. When a girl is ready to be married, then maybe she will talk or make some conversation in order to know the boy before she gets married. But they don't have boyfriends. So my two eldest daughters go to school together, they come home together, they are friends and they walk together. When they come back from school, one of them may go to the kitchen and do her chores and one does her homework and so on, but they don't go out on dates. My son is more active than my daughters. He has some friends, but not girlfriends. I don't know whether he's hiding them from me. He goes with his Canadian friends to the school, then he comes back and usually I don't allow him to go out at night.

A person's colour is different here. It has its advantages and at the same time it has its disadvantages. Maybe something that you believe is different from what others believe. So firstly what I told my children is to respect everyone–what a person likes, what a person believes. In Somalia, my children didn't have any experience with other kinds of people. They thought all the people were Muslims, all the people pray to one God or something like that. Back home in our country, when other people come from other countries, for example, when white people come to us, we respect them and we treat them as our guests, but here they become what they call black people and coloured people. My children realized that they heard a word that they never ever heard before, which is "negro." They said, "Mummy, what does 'negro' mean?" They don't have any idea. I think that they feel an inferiority complex. They associate with many people now. They have many ideas. They know many things about the world. They have friends from Asia, from Latin America, from Europe. They have more knowledge now than before–very international. It has been an advantage and disadvantage. Sometimes while the teacher is explaining history classes, they talk about slavery. Well, who were the slaves? The black people. My daughter Amina hates even to hear anything bad about the black people, so sometimes she says, "No, we were born free. Sometimes they say the people think we were slaves, but no, we were not."

After arriving in Canada and going through the immigration process from inquiry to hearing, the refugee hearing board established my status as a refugee. I applied for landed immigrant status. My problems started from there. After waiting some time to get my landed immigrant status, I was told that as I have a sick child, I am not getting the landed immigrant status because of the sick child. The only option I have is either to wait five years or to leave the country. I was astonished and shocked. I never realized it. That caused the family a lot of problems.

At the hearings, they saw Hibaq and they accepted her condition. My lawyer saw her and the refugee hearing board saw her and they granted refugee status for all the members of the family, including the sick child. There were also contradicting views on this issue. The family physician said that immigration sometimes needs medical information about the refugee that they don't know what to do with. My lawyer told me also that as long as the child is here in Canada and was accepted as a refugee, there should not be any problem in getting landed immigrant status. The disease my daughter is suffering from is common in Canada, and they have an organization and a school that looks after that. The school there has so many Canadian children, some of them in much poorer health than my daughter.

The doctors have told me that this kind of disease cannot be treated because they don't have a medicine for it so far, but my daughter is paralysed, she needs a lot of physical exercise that needs equipment. That is something material that I cannot afford to buy and that I don't have.

A centre that helps handicapped children has been helping me, and now I have a chair. My daughter needs some electronic things, as she can neither move nor write–that's the problem–and she cannot get it. I welcome anyone who can help her. I think the major problem right now is the house. This house is not designed for a handicapped child.

When you first arrive at the border, you don't know anything about this government or this country. So the Somali people, the community, and the friends you know are the first people who help you. When I came to the border, some Somali friends picked me up. They took me to their house and later they took me to the social services. The social services told me I had to wait. They will send someone to make a home visit, and that person took a week to come. It was December, it was terribly cold. They sent a cheque for the basic food allowance, and later on when I found the apartment, they provided the rent of the house and the food allowance.

We left Somalia because of security, but in this building, we don't have security. Every hour the alarm goes on. If you see how many locks people have on their doors, you will be surprised. We are scared and I've never slept more than one hour. Whenever I hear something, a noise, I have to look. It is really a bad environment, this Willow Ridge Metro Housing. We are still living in fear. My children call it Hell House.

For me the only blessing now is my children. I lost my husband, my country, my property, everything. The only thing I worry about is their safety, their education, and their happiness.

I'm not working now because of my status. The work permit I have has a lot of conditions with it. It is sort of a closed work permit. The only jobs I can get would pay even less than welfare.

I went to Somali University and got my first degree in economics. I worked for the Ministry of Treasury and Finance for a long, long time.

I have not taken any upgrading, training, or education and this is because of my status. When you go to any college or educational institution, they will ask you about your status. If you don't have landed immigrant status or if you are not Canadian, you can't go. If I had landed immigrant status, I would upgrade or retrain because I spent approximately twenty years of my life in school, and if that means nothing, I am going to start again. That's why I spent so many years in school–to improve my life.

I have to decide whether or not to let my daughter, Hibaq, have surgery. If she doesn't have surgery, she will suffer a lot of spinal pain and will have to lie in bed for the rest of her life. And if she has surgery, she may die. It is too big a risk. It is a big decision. I needed time to think about that, so I explained it to my eldest children because I need help in making that decision.

When I told my eldest daughter, she started to cry. I talked to my second oldest daughter at the same time. She said, "Mummy, I don't know what to say." She said go ahead. So I started to think about it. It would be better than lying all the time in bed, so we decided to have the surgery. Nevertheless, I am still feeling very painful because if my daughter dies in surgery, I will feel guilty because I said go ahead.

It is a big decision. It is a time when I need my husband to help me make the decision. You can't do it by yourself, so sometimes you pray a lot. I pray a lot. I need help from my friends and some religious people. But I still feel sad.

The doctor said it is up to me. He gave me this booklet and no more information. My daughter will be in intensive care for at least ten to fifteen days. I must be with her at that time. If she is going to pass away, I would like to spend the last minute of her life with her.

Some Somalis are helping me, but I have a little kid who will be three years old this April. She needs somebody to look after her all the time. Who will manage this? That is the whole problem.

My husband was not only my husband, he was my best friend. He was my teacher and sometimes he was like a parent to me because he was fourteen years older than me. All the time we made all decisions together.

I am homesick all the time. Sometimes I pray that my people will agree and make some difference in my country and we can go back and have a life because you can't imagine the life that I left behind. I miss my husband, I miss my parents, I miss my country, I miss all my friends.

When I was separated from Amina, Filsan, and Fahiye for a year and a half, you can't imagine how worried I was. We are all together now. Whether we are living in poverty or not, we are living, and we hope one day we will be successful. We know that there is no place better than home and now my children and I know that.

My eldest daughter will graduate from high school in the coming year. If she wants to go to college or university, we don't have any money. Back home we were not worried about that because university was free. But here the people who study also have money, but we don't have money, so they may go to work in order to survive or something like that. We are remembering that we lost a very big opportunity, and we hope that God will bring us back.

My husband was a very educated person. He was a very respected and responsible man. Everybody who knew him knows it's true. He was responsible to the community and at the same time to his family.

In some regions, there was a lot of corruption. He was a member of Parliament. Those who are corrupt have a lot of money, but we do not, because my husband was a very nationalistic person. He didn't participate in the corruption that was going on at that time. He was really a very wise man, he was a very responsible man. I miss him a lot.

I am moderate. I am in the middle. I believe in my God, in my religion.

I am setting up a group to help Somali women who are in a similar situation. Somali women and children are the victims. We are not struggling for power. We do not care about power, but we have the right to live in a peaceful way. The Somali women are the victims of that war. They rape them, they kill them, they kill their children, they die of starvation. These men are destroying women and children, so I want to speak their language to tell them that they are the gangs who are destroying our country, killing our husbands, and raping our women. Even though I am a single parent, some of the people who live here are not single parents. Sometimes I feel ashamed to say that I am a single parent. They think that I am a prostitute or something like that. I think a lot about the women who are suffering in this civil war. We need some organizations and Somali women who will stand up and talk about what is going on here. I want to go there and tell them that it is the gangs who are destroying our country because of their personal interests. They are the ones who sent us out to kill us, to make us starve, and everything like that.

I was trying to make some arrangements for the orphaned children in Somalia. There are lot of orphaned children. I was looking for some people who can help me. I can feel because I am now in that position, so I know how deeply sad they are. I am feeling very sad about what is going on there, so I will try my best to make some connections between Canada and Somalia.

Fahiye Abdi Home was a very nice, sunny place. It was a decent, good place. We used to live in a really big house. My dad was a very successful man. Back there the education was very good. We used to live in a great place, we knew everybody who lived there.

Life in Canada feels like hell, I guess. It's a very cold place here. When I first came from Somalia, I didn't know how cold it was.

The white people don't treat the black people very well, as if they are slaves or something. It feels very unhappy. It is like hell for black people. At school when they see someone is black, when they see someone from Somalia, they think that that person is very poor or that they are homeless or something like that.

School is going pretty well. I get a good education. Back in your homeland, you understand everyone else. The first time I came here, I couldn't understand one thing that the teacher was saying, but you catch up with the language and stuff. But people you work with in school treat you like a dog or something.

I am in grade eight. I have four or five Canadian friends–two black Canadians and the others are white.

Amina Abdi When I lived in my country, we lived a very good life. My father was working, we lived in a big house with big gardens and trees. We were never scared of anything. You could go wherever you want. Now when you want to go somewhere, you feel scared. But we were never scared of anything. We didn't have a problem with the language. Everything was in our language and we understood everything.

I lived with my family in Somalia until I was seventeen years old. I can say I had a wonderful time because I never had any problems like the ones I had for the last two years.

The civil war broke out in the capital city of my country on 30 December 1990. It was Sunday at one o'clock p.m. when I heard the first noise. After four days, we couldn't stay at home because the war kept coming nearer. On Wednesday, 2 January, we went to a little town near Mogadishu. We lived with my uncle for fifteen days. Then we went to another city and we paid to stay in a house. We were expecting the war to be finished and then we could go back to Mogadishu, but everything got worse.

After that my father decided to take my brother, my sister, and me to Canada because my mother, my aunt, and my three little sisters lived in Canada and my father wanted us to live with them. To come to Canada, we had to go to another country because there was no transportation working at that time in Somalia. Besides, there was no peace.

On 27 February 1991, we arrived in Kenya by boat. We were almost in a little city named Mulind when suddenly the boat crashed against stone or something. The bottom of the boat was torn. The water was coming in fast from the side of the boat and it was getting full.

All the men started to throw everything out of the boat to save the people. A few men took a little lifeboat and went to the city to get help. After a few hours, they came back with just their lifeboat and they told us they didn't get any help from that city.

While they were away, the rest of us were yelling and burning things like sheets to let the people in the city know that we needed their help, but nobody cared about us. There were many people coming around the beach and taking our stuff because when we threw them into the sea, the water carried them to shore. My father was one of those who were throwing stuff off the boat and trying to save the people for at least a little longer. Time was running out.

The men were getting tired and the water was coming in more and more. At that time we realized that we were not getting any help from anyone, so people decided to save themselves and whoever they were responsible for. The problem was that most of the people didn't know how to swim so, if a family had maybe six or eight people and only one or two of them knew how to swim, they had to take the others one by one. Besides, there wasn't that much time. As a family, we were five people—my father, my sister, my brother, my aunt, and I. Only my father knew how to swim, so he decided to take care of my sister and my brother because they were the youngest. My aunt and I swam by ourselves because my father had no choice. He couldn't do anything else.

I had a little beauty case that I hid when the people started throwing the things out of the boat. There were important things in it like my mother's gold and my sister's and mine, too. My father told me to put that bag on my chest and try to swim. I held the bag with my hands and jumped out of the boat because I had no idea about swimming. Besides, I was totally confused and scared. I didn't even know what I was doing. When I jumped out of the boat, I went under the water. After I went up and down two or three times, I saw a woman carrying a baby on her back and holding a barrel with her hands. I caught the barrel with the woman and let the bag go. At that time I wasn't thinking about gold or anything else except my life. I never thought I was going to live. I went back to the boat and sat on the edge of the boat. I didn't see any of my family and I didn't know who was alive and who wasn't. After a little while, my cousin came back and told me that he had saved my sister and my brother after he found them holding a pillow and yelling for help. I realized, in that case, that my father was dead. My cousin took me to the shore and I found my sister and brother on the beach.

Since we left the city of Kismaayo, we never had enough sleep because the boat was so crowded and we didn't have enough space to sleep. Many people who didn't even know how to swim jumped out of the boat and they started to catch the others. When I asked my sister and brother when they last saw our father, they told me that when he was taking them to land, a man caught my sister. After a little fighting, my father took her away from the man. By the time he saved my sister from the man, a woman came and grabbed my father's neck like a snake. That was when my sister and brother last saw my father.

Then I was sure that my father and aunt were not alive, and I was responsible for finding their bodies and taking care of my sister and brother. I gave them some milk and bread from some people. When they heard about our boat, they really did the best they could. Many people were even saved by them. I wished that they had known earlier about us. I was looking around until I found my father's and aunt's bodies.

The Italian community and some other people, who were mostly Muslim (which is my religion), took care of us that night and the next day. All of the people who survived were taken to a refugee camp, which was located in another city called Mombasa. We went to the camp at eight o'clock p.m. We stayed there that night and left the next day in the afternoon when my uncle took us to Nairobi.

We lived in Nairobi for four months. Although we were better off than those who lived in the camp, we still weren't happy about being in Kenya at all. The four months we lived there seemed like four years and it seemed so to my mother as well. One of the reasons we didn't like living in Nairobi was that they didn't want the refugees to live anywhere else in Kenya except the refugee camps, so when they found anyone in the cities, they took them to the camps or returned them to Somalia. It was almost eight o'clock in the evening and I was getting ready to pray when suddenly three Kenyan army officers came into our house and asked us if we had any Kenyan documents, which we didn't have. How could we? They told us that they were going to take us to jail, and they did. Thank God we were free in three hours before they locked us in. That was the first time I have ever been in jail. Thank God I was not a criminal.

On 12 July 1991, I came to Canada. I am in high school and I would like to be a nurse when I finish my education. The biggest problem that I have with my education is the language. Although I am better than I was last year, I still don't know enough English.

The people who get the highest marks get the best education in Canada or maybe in every other country. It is very hard to get a high mark if you don't know enough English and that can affect your education or your future. Even if you never skip any classes or are never late at school or are never absent except if you are sick and even if you do everything that your teachers tell you to do, someone else who does all of those things can get a higher mark than you do. What can happen is that he or she can do perfectly on the tests, exams, and homework, which you would probably have problems in understanding. It also depends on how helpful your teacher is.

I am not feeling very happy. Many things changed, like school. The culture is different. Sometimes you do something and the people think that you are wrong or that you do not know anything. I think it is hard to understand everything when you come to a new country, and it is hard to understand the people.

I was much happier in my country than in Canada because I didn't have any problems. Now we are immigrants. We don't even have landed immigrant status because of my younger sister who is six years old. She is sick. It is not fair for them to say "If she is sick, you can't be a landed immigrant." It is not fair. Anyway, I hope that one day we will be happy and that we will go back to my country. We are better off than the people who live in Mogadishu now, so I am happy about that, but one day I would like to go back to my country.

I am eighteen. I am in grade ten. I am not working because I have to learn English. Now I study at school. Even if I wanted to work, I can't because I don't have a social insurance number. I don't have landed immigrant status or anything like that. Even when you want to get a job, there are a lot of situations where they ask if you have worked before. When you look at the sheet, you must answer no, no, no, to everything. Last week there was a sheet for summer jobs in our school. I took that sheet and I wanted to fill it out, but I couldn't because my answer would be no to every question, so how could I work?

Now I have to study, but I don't know how the future will be. I still have not decided anything. I would like to be a doctor, a lawyer, or even a secretary. I like working in an office. If I was in my country, I would have finished high school and I would be in college or university, but now I have to start high school. I hope it will be okay.

There was a civil war in our country. We lived in the capital and then we left. We rode a boat and the boat sank near Kenya, and then my daddy died and other people almost died, but we were lucky that we didn't die. We saw a lot of difficulties and also money problems. We are not very happy. I was the oldest and I didn't know anything. I did not know anything about the new country. It was just me, my younger sister, and my brother. I was the oldest, so I had to take care of them and also I needed help too. Anyway, that was a long time ago. I told them good things. I was trying to make them happy. When we were in Kenya, I thought that my mother lived in heaven, that she lived in a house bigger than our house. You believe it will be beautiful, but now I know everything.

This building is the worst place we've lived in as long as I've lived in Canada. When we were moving here, we thought it was a nice house because it is big and it doesn't have stairs, which is good for my younger sister, who has muscular dystrophy. That is the reason why we moved here, but now we don't want to live here. There is a lot of drugs, a lot of bad people. Even when you want to go downstairs you feel scared, you can't ride in the elevators. Sometimes the elevators don't work. My younger sister is disabled, so we must take her on the elevator. One day we couldn't get the elevator and my mother carried her and we used the stairs. This building is not even safe. There are a lot of fire-alarms. You can't even sleep at night. I think they just play with the fire-alarms. There is not even a real fire.

Hodan Abdi   My name is Hodan. I am eight years old. I like Canada, but I miss my home. It was really beautiful, but since the civil war started, it is all crushed up and I can't go back because I have nowhere to sleep, so I came to Canada. I used to sleep in a baby bed in my mum and dad's bedroom. It was really beautiful in their bedroom. And now it is all crushed up and it is all bricks.

There were lots of plants there. There used to be apples and lots of growing gardens, and it was beautiful. There used to be a fence and me and my brother used to run around there and play tag. There were lots of plants. It was like a jungle. And upstairs there were plants. It was so beautiful. I think about it every day.

Here in our apartment there is no backyard, there is no fence, and there are no plants in here. I really miss it, but I'm glad I came to Canada because I would have been one of those starving children over there.

I miss my dad. He was a very handsome gentleman, and he sure had a lot of money. My mother used to be a bank manager. My father used to talk to a lot of people and I knew where he worked. He was a nice gentleman who came from a good family. He used to have a car and he drove us every Friday. He was a very, very handsome gentleman.

I am in grade three. School is not that bad and there are children there who came from a country because of war, too, just like me. And I really feel sorry for them, just like me. I have a lot of friends at school, but they are not actually that nice.

When we talk about our daddies, I feel really sad and I feel so sad that I can hardly cry. I told my teacher that I didn't have a dad and she said that you can talk about mums, and I said it is okay, I can talk about how he was. He was a nice gentleman. She said it is okay if you want to draw a picture and talk about it. It is okay. I said I'll draw a picture. And then I started to cry and I went to the bathroom and I stopped crying. I thought that if my dad is dead, I still have my mummy and my family. In my journal I wrote that in my country, my dad used to take us everywhere and he used to take us to the forest and through this bridge.

I feel very happy that we are in Canada because there is food and lots of people who could help me. There are teachers and food and snow to play with. In my country there was never snow. And I like Canada because it is very beautiful, and there are not too many people.

In Somalia there is one thing I like–the sun. You don't have to wear jackets or boots. I can wear shorts, or t-shirts, or anything. There are no people who will steal you or kidnap you. You can go to your friend's house two blocks away. Everybody is nice, except for the soldiers.

I want to be a lawyer because you help solve mysteries if people are innocent or guilty and it is really fun helping people who may be innocent or guilty.

The Somali Community

Edward Opoku-Dapaah

The flight of Somalis to Canada began in the late 1970s after the 1976 removal of discriminatory clauses in Canadian immigration laws. The influx gained momentum from 1980 to 1990 when Somalia fell under Siad Barre's military rule. During this decade, political repression against targeted clans and violent acts by military units and individuals in the national armed forces[1] resulted in the flight of Somalis to destinations within and beyond Africa. Many of the Somalis who came to Canada testified that they experienced violent persecution, mass repression, and torture.[2]

Approximately 25,000 Somalis have settled in Toronto within the past twelve years. Toronto's multicultural nature, comparatively better economic opportunities, and the large Somali community have made the city a popular choice for resettlement by Somali refugees. Most fled Somalia and found their way to Toronto first, seeking refugee status once they were here in Canada. Refugee claims by Somalis rose from a mere thirty-one in 1985 to 3,503 within the first six months of 1991. The total number of Somalis who applied for refugee status from within Canada between 1985 and 1991 was 12,957. This made Somalis the most numerous among the African refugees coming to Canada. The substantial increase in Somali refugee claims between 1988 and 1991 was commensurate with the heightened repression, famine, and resultant displacement that occurred in Somalia during that period.

Somalis who sought refugee status from within Canada waited in the refugee backlog for two or more years before completing the inland refugee determination process. This prolonged the refugee application period and its attendant anxieties. In 1989, there were 2,613 Somalis in the refugee backlog.[3] Even after successfully completing the process, applicants could wait as long as two years before receiving permanent status. While they waited, refugee claimants were not allowed to apply for and change their immigration status. Claimants received permanent residential status only when the application process was completed with a positive outcome. Also, claimants could not leave the country since travelling abroad jeopardized the refugee claim. They were required to inform immigration authorities whenever they relocated.

Most Somalis in Toronto are within the age range of eighteen to forty. It is mostly young adults who are able to embark on the stressful flight to destinations beyond Africa. More than half are female. The presettlement educational attainments of Somalis in Canada is moderately high; about one-fourth of them finished high school or more. A large proportion of Somali youth are enrolled in schools and colleges.

The picture is different, however, for those who are between the ages of twenty-one to thirty-five. Only a small percentage of those in this age category are currently pursuing academic studies or professional development. Factors affecting academic pursuits include lack of educational counselling and financial assistance. Government grants and educational loans have not been available to those who intended to pursue higher education or upgrade skills. In almost all Canadian provinces, even after residential status is granted, landed refugees are required to work at least one year before they are eligible for grants.[4]

Somalis' active participation in employment-related programs, such as skills upgrading and retraining, have been hampered by the lack of information. New immigrants' access to retraining in Ontario's public educational system and federally- and provincially-funded programs is impeded by institutional barriers such as lack of publicity, entrance requirements, tuition fees, prerequisites, and full-time attendance requirements.[5] Some training programs have stringent prerequisites such as Ontario or Canadian experience and language proficiency, which Somali refugees find hard to meet.

Somali women have lower educational achievements compared to Somali men, and they are less inclined to pursue studies. Situational barriers related to child care, language proficiency, scheduling, and financial cost impede Somali women's education. Socio-cultural forces have also impeded their efforts to engage in studies; besides their paid work outside the home, women also perform most of the domestic duties, which leave them very little time to pursue even part-time studies. Wives' career plans may require approval from their husbands, which is not always forthcoming.

The fact that the Somalis' prior socio-cultural and economic norms diverge from mainstream Canadian norms and that they encounter barriers in pursuing academic studies or employment-related training programs limit their effective participation in Canadian society. Somalis come from a Third World nation that is on the threshold of industrial development. Their exposure to advanced technology and industrial culture is very low. Moreover, in the case of those with prior academic and professional accomplishments, their qualifications and related work experiences were obtained in foreign institutions whose professional training methods differ from those in Canada. These circumstances make it crucial that those with prior academic and professional credentials take refresher courses and skills upgrading so they can utilize their qualifications in Canada. Those who have no academic qualifications or skills that can be transferred to the Canadian economic context need to pursue occupational training or education of some sort.

Many Somali refugees have a low proficiency in English. This reflects the fact that English is neither the official language nor a widely used one in Somalia. Even those who are highly educated and proficient in English need to undertake language classes to acquire a proficiency comparable to that of the average Canadian. Somali men have a higher English proficiency rate than

Somali women. The disparity stems from socio-cultural practices in Somalia that favour education for men more so than women. The determination to improve proficiency in English has been hampered by inadequate access to language training programs and the insensitivity of existing programs to the cultural background of Somalis.

The Somali refugee community is concentrated in northern metropolitan Toronto. Approximately half the community live in the suburb of Etobicoke.[6] Somalis are also concentrated in North York, Malton, York, and Scarborough. A large percentage of them live in rented accommodations, particularly in high-rise apartments. The choice of area of settlement is influenced mostly by the desire to live closer to fellow Somalis. Group tenancy–that is, a number of people sharing a common apartment–is very popular. This is the result of the continuous arrival of Somalis in Toronto and the lack of affordable housing for refugees who live on subsistence allowances.[7] Judging by the Canadian norm of one person per room, Somalis in Toronto are overcrowded in their residential units.

The population's lifestyle is heavily influenced by prior socio-cultural values. The preference for living close to other Somalis is an extension of communal living among kin and extended relatives in Somalia. Living close together has also enabled them to create an island of familiarity in a new and complex environment.

Age is highly respected, and the elderly exercise considerable influence on the young. Marriage ceremonies follow strict Muslim laws. Marital roles follow the traditional pattern in which wives are responsible for child care and domestic duties. Children are constantly reminded of the traditional way of doing things and the importance of knowing their heritage. The influence of Islamic religious teachings pervades their daily activities. In spite of such strong attachments to cultural values, adherence to Canadian norms are also enforced.

Individual Somalis find it difficult to participate in mainstream Canadian society. Instead, they are drawn into networks of primary relationships with kin and other members of the African community. Friendship ties are very strong and involve a high degree of commitment. Inadequate access to settlement-related facilities, stereotyping in the media, and other social and economic disadvantages have fostered reactive solidarity among Somalis. People tend to limit their social activities not only among their own compatriots but also within their immediate geographic confines.

Several factors have led to this. First, they are unfamiliar with the Canadian environment. The differences between the socio-cultural practices of their homeland and those of Canada have placed them at a disadvantage. As a result, individuals are unable to establish channels of communication with members of the wider community. Secondly, those with limited or no proficiency in English find it hard to communicate with the general public. Thirdly, participation in employment and educational pursuits, which can bring them into regular contact with others, is affected by institutional barriers, such as delays in getting permits to work or study. Fourthly, when Somalis arrive in Canada as refugee claimants, many of them do not receive any orientation about formal and informal institutional structures and prevailing social norms in Canada, which hampers their ability to interact with other Canadians. All these factors, particularly the lack of orientation and (in the case of those who were caught in the refugee backlog) the uncertainty about the outcome of refugee applications, have impeded the development of interpersonal relations and friendships with native-born Canadians.

The current unemployment rate among the Somali community is approximately 40 per cent. This is partly attributable to the generally high level of unemployment in Toronto's depressed economy. Since the late 1980s, the recession in Canada has slowed down economic activity. Industrial employment has declined as manufacturing has become more capital intensive and the economy more service oriented. Under these conditions, the growth of per capita income in Canada depends on skilled workers, capital investment, technology, and international markets for more efficient production.[8] Somali refugees' limited exposure to industry, lack of technical skills, limited English proficiency, and inadequate opportunities to obtain upgrading or retraining place them at a disadvantage within Canada's job market.

Three patterns are discernible in the economic characteristics of the Somali refugee community. First, a few do not have work permits, so they depend on government assistance. Second, the majority with landed immigrant status have work permits, but are compelled to work as cleaners, flyer distributors, parking-lot attendants, taxi drivers, and couriers. People with prior educational qualifications and work experience are unable to get jobs on the basis of these achievements. Moreover, employers demand Canadian work experience and adequate language skill. Discrimination has also prevented those with work permits and higher academic qualifications from getting preferred jobs. Since they have no access to upgrading and retraining facilities to help them obtain desirable jobs, they are compelled to seek employment in fields that marginalize their potential. Third, many Somali refugees who have work permits cannot find work. Unemployment among Somalis stems from the fact that Canada's advanced industrial society has no room for informal economic activities, such as petty trading, peddling, tailoring, cloth weaving, craft work, subsistence agriculture, and pastoral activities that employed such people when they were in Somalia. Somali men have a higher employment rate than Somali women, which reflects men's greater English proficiency, higher educational background, and males' traditional role as the breadwinner in the family. The average income is approximately $10,000, indicating that most Somali refugees live well below the poverty line.

Somali refugees in Toronto have formed numerous community associations to cater to their needs. The most established ones are the Somali Community Association of Etobicoke, Somali Immigrant Aid, Somali-Canadian Women's Association, Somali Islamic Society, and the Ogaden Somalis Association. The

Somali-Canadian Women's Association has been primarily concerned with addressing gender-specific problems facing its members. There are also agencies that mobilize relief aid to the Somalis back home, for example, the Western Somali Relief Organization and the Somali Aid Working Group. The associations provide settlement-related services, such as orientation for new arrivals, referrals to government departments, employment and family counselling, translation services, day care, and English classes.[9] The associations also provide entertainment through social get-togethers, annual dinners, and dances.

Limited financial resources available to the groups restrict their ability to function effectively as care-givers for the Somali community. Some community members have frequently alleged that various Somali associations perpetuate clan factionalism through their overt allegiance to particular clans. This affects the image of the associations within the community and restricts their ability to raise funds from the Toronto community to support programs. The associations lack professional expertise to help clients with complex problems, such as psychological trauma resulting from displacement, family breakdown, and family abuse. Also, the presence of many groups performing similar functions sets the stage for competition and rivalry.

A small number of community members express satisfaction with their life in Canada in terms of residential status, an improved socio-economic situation, and the opportunity to bring over family members from Africa. Most Somali refugees are dissatisfied because of their reduced socio-economic status, the prevalence of discrimination, and feelings of homesickness.

Somalis in Toronto have retained their traditional cultural values to a considerable degree. The internalization of Canadian norms by Somalis is very low; adherence to Canadian values is made based on circumstantial demands or when it is deemed crucial for meeting personal motives. Their social interaction has not progressed beyond their primary (kin and co-ethnic) level of social participation; interaction with the Canadian-born is limited.

Their inability to blend easily into Canada's mainstream culture and their residential concentration in certain areas have frequently engendered racism from a section of the community. For those who still see Canada as primarily a European Judeo-Christian nation, Somalis have become an irritant.[10] There have been occasional denunciations describing the status of Somalis as refugees as "bogus" and "fraudulent" in leading dailies. The most graphic example was a five-part series on Canada's immigration system, in the *Toronto Sun* (20–24 September 1992), which questioned the legitimacy of Somali refugee claims.[11]

The continuous turmoil in their homeland and the media's persistent depiction of it as a land of misery, chaos, and total disaster affects the emotional stability and self-perception of this refugee community. Interviews conducted in 1992 revealed that Somalis find it difficult to concentrate on their lives in Canada due to the deaths of relatives.[12] Healing and coping take a long time. Somalis who are working find it difficult to concentrate on their jobs due to the personal problems they face and the memories of chaos and death that grip their country daily.[13] Somali families have been torn apart; families in Toronto are single parents with "reconstituted family members," that is, extended family groupings of survivors.[14] Somalis encounter major problems in bringing their families here.

These social, economic, and psychological characteristics of Somalis do not constitute integration into Canadian society but marginalization. Marginalization occurs when refugees are sidelined onto the periphery of Canadian society without participating fully in the prevailing social, economic, and political activities to their advantage.[15] As a result, they can live neither according to their own standards nor attain those of the host country.[16]

Overall, Somalis constitute the largest African community in Toronto. There are many enthusiastic and dynamic young people who are trying to improve their own situation in Canada while hoping that the situation back home in Somalia will improve enough so that some day they will be able to return.

Notes

1. D. Compagnon, "Political Decay in Somalia: From Personal Rule to Warlordism," *Refuge* Vol. 12, No. 5 (1992), pp. 8–13.
2. Joan Simalchik, "Somali Torture Survivors in Canada," *Refuge* Vol. 12, No. 5 (1992), p. 27.
3. H. Adelman, "Canadian Refugee Policy in the Postwar Period: An Analysis," *Refugee Policy: Canada and the United States*, edited by H. Adelman, (North York, Ont., 1991), pp. 172-223.
4. Edward Opoku-Dapaah, *A Survey of Available Funding for Post-Secondary Education in Canada* (North York, Ont., 1982).
5. P. Cummings et al., *Access! Task Force on Access to Professions and Trades in Ontario* (Toronto, 1989).
6. C. McInnes, "A Home Called Dixon," *The Globe and Mail* (28 November 1992), Section D.
7. Ibid.
8. Alan Simmons, "Consequences of International Migration: The Canadian Experience," unpublished manuscripted, Centre for Research on Latin America and the Caribbean, York University (North York, Ont., n.d.).
9. Edward Opoku-Dapaah, *Inventory of African Community Groups in Toronto* (North York, Ont., 1993).
10. McInnes.
11. D. Stoffman, "The High Cost of Our Refugee System," *Toronto Star* (September 1992), p. A19.
12. K. Warner, "A Somali Working Manual for Canadian Educators and Social Service Workers," unpublished manuscript, Ontario Institute for Studies in Education (Toronto, n.d.).
13. Ibid.
14. McInnes.

15. Edward Opoku-Dapaah, "Integration of African Refugees in Canada: An Explanatory Model," unpublished manuscript, Centre for Research on Latin America and the Caribbean, York University (North York, Ont., n.d.).
16. T. Kuhlman, "The Integration of Refugees in Developing Countries: A Research Model," *Journal of Refugee Studies*, Vol. 4, No. 1 (1991), p. 19.

Further Reading

Abella, Irving, and Harold Troper. *None Is Too Many: Canada and the Jews of Europe, 1933–1948*. Toronto: Lester & Orpen Dennys, 1983.

Adelman, Howard, ed. *Refugee Policy: Canada and the United States*. North York, Ont: York Lanes Press, 1991.

Dirks, Gerald. *Canada's Refugee Policy: Indifference or Opportunism?* Montreal: McGill-Queen's Press, 1977.

Hawkins, Freda. *Canada and Immigration: Public Policy and Public Concern* (2nd ed.). Toronto: University of Toronto Press, 1988.

Malarek, Victor. *Haven's Gate: Canada's Refugee Fiasco*. Toronto: Macmillan Canada 1987.

Marrus, Michael. *The Unwanted: European Refugees in the Twentieth Century*. New York: Oxford University Press, 1985.

Matas, David, with Ilana Simon. *Closing the Doors: The Future of Refugee Protection*. Toronto: Summerhill Press, 1989.

Plaut, Gunther. *Refugee Determination in Canada: Proposals for a New System*. Ottawa: Employment and Immigration Canada, 1985.

Zolberg, Aristide R., Astri Suhrke, and Sergio Aguayo. *Escape from Violence: The Refugee Crisis in the Developing World*. New York: Oxford University Press, 1989.

Acknowledgments

Safe Haven is a book, but it is also an exhibition produced by the MHSO as the inaugural show in the new Heritage Gallery of Canada's Peoples at the Royal Ontario Museum. This gallery is a joint venture between the MHSO and the ROM and will feature exhibitions produced by the MHSO and the ROM on the diverse cultural communities within Canada.

The leadership provided to this innovative partnership by Dr Paul Robert Magocsi, Director of the MHSO, and Dr John McNeill, Director of the ROM, must be cited at the outset. Liza Samuel has been a driving force behind the new gallery, and a friend and colleague on the ROM Board of Trustees.

A working committee was established to oversee the completion of the new gallery, co-ordinate joint aspects of exhibit production, and plan the opening. From the ROM, Jean Lavery, Associate Director of Public Programs, and Margo Welch, Head of Exhibitions, worked with optimism and flexibility in forging a closer ROM/MHSO association. This tradition is being maintained and reshaped by Jean Lavery's successor, Florence Silver.

From the MHSO, the partnership and the Safe Haven project were guided and nurtured by Carl Thorpe, Associate Director, who assumed on more than one occasion the role of troubleshooter. A special thanks must go to former MHSO board member, Dr Harold Troper, of OISE, who contributed the title essay of the book, and his historical expertise and moral support throughout, and to the MHSO's Chairman, Dr Milton Israel, of the University of Toronto, for providing the book's preface and considerable research assistance on the Tamil community.

From the beginning, *Safe Haven* was a team effort. Research Associates Eva Marha, Carlos Piña, Jennifer Khong, Sujata Ramachandran, and Edward Opoku-Dapaah were responsible for establishing community contacts, locating and recommending an appropriate family, and assembling community advisers. They carried out family interviews, and researched the family and community profiles. Their commitment to *Safe Haven* was unflagging.

The MHSO commissioned photographer Vincenzo Pietropaulo to assemble profiles of the families and their respective communities. In addition to producing a striking visual document, Vince was an active link with the families and the communities at large.

Safe Haven is also an array of special activities sponsored by the Czech, Chilean, Vietnamese, Sri Lankan Tamil, and Somali communities at the ROM during the run of the exhibition. The professional and volunteer efforts of many people and organizations were necessary to make this multifaceted project a reality. The community advisers planned and managed special activities at the ROM. They were also a source of support and encouragement throughout. Thanks must go to: Anna Mach and Peter Munk, Director of the Czechoslovak Association of Canada (Toronto branch); Duberlis Ramos, Director of the Hispanic Council of Metropolitan Toronto, Mariela Morales, of Co-op Arauco, and Maria Angelica Nuñez Enriquez of the Centre for Spanish-Speaking Peoples; also Gabriel Parada, of the Refugee Information Centre, and Joan Simalchik, of the Canadian Centre for Victims of Torture; Michael Dang, Pham, Thê Trung, Tom Pham and Paul Truong who, with the Vietnamese Professional Association, co-ordinated the involvement of numerous individuals and organizations from the Vietnamese-Canadian community; Rajaratnam Subramanian, Director of the Tamil Eelam Society of Canada, S. Gnaneswaren, Siva Segaran, Selvam Sridas, and the Academy of Tamil Arts and Technology; Faduma Abdi and the Somali Community Association of Etobicoke.

Valerie Ahwee applied her copy-editing skills to the manuscript. M.J. Sicard took the manuscript in hand and donated many volunteer days of computer services. Acknowledgement is due as well to Carolyn Braunlich, who volunteered her time to the manuscript. The project benefited by the earlier volunteer contributions of Deborah Kaplan, who transcribed many of the original interviews. Throughout, Andrew Israel was an efficient and tireless research assistant. Arul Aruliah of the Centre for Refugee Studies at York University provided the profile of the Sri Lankan Tamil community, drawing on his extensive knowledge of the Tamil refugees in Canada.

The MHSO owes an extraordinary debt to the five families who agreed to be the subject of this book and exhibition. They are: Marta and Ivan Straznicky and their children, Marta, Ivan, Magdalene, John, David, Lenka, and Michal; Maria Angelica Nuñez Enriquez, and Gabriela, Fernan, and Claudio; Pham, Thê Trung and Thai, Ni Phan with Hieu (Daniel) and Hai (David); Indira and Siva Segaran and their children, Mirunalini, Vasee-haran, and Ketharini, and their grandfather, S.N. Rajah; Faduma Abdi and Amina, with Filsan, Fahiye, Hibaq, Hodan, and Warsan.

The families gave their time and trust to the project in the hopes that their stories would reach the broader Canadian public and encourage understanding and tolerance for refugees today.

The Safe Haven Exhibition

Openings are exciting. They are like new births. They can even be fun. But they should mean something.

Tonight's event is more than an opening for a particular show. It is also the first public result of a new partnership established about a year ago between the Multicultural History Society of Ontario, an institution dedicated to the study of all the peoples who live in our country, and the Royal Ontario Museum, part of whose mandate is to study all aspects of this land called Canada.

We are very pleased that this partnership has gotten off to an excellent start. It would not have happened had it not been for the foresight of the ROM's director, Dr John McNeill; our resident curator, Elizabeth McLuhan; and most especially, Elizabeth Samuel or Liza, as we all fondly know her, whose generosity made possible the physical space that houses this and future exhibits. In many ways, tonight marks the inauguration of an exercise that shows just what two public institutions–in this case, the MHSO and the ROM–can do when they pool their intellectual and financial resources. I should say human resources as well, since I think you, as I am, must be impressed with the genuine charm and efficiency of the ROM's staff, from the moment they greeted us at the entrance until we reached this rotunda.

But now, let's get to the heart of the matter. What are we here for tonight? To go somewhere on a cold November evening? To fulfil, pro forma, the obligation of responding to an invitation we received? To enjoy some food and company?

I would say we are here tonight because we have a duty. As Canadians, we have a duty to confront some serious issues facing our country.

Since World War II, and in particular since the late 1960s, Canada has experienced a period of enormous growth. Part of that growth was demographic. In short, we needed people to inhabit and work this vast land. So we opened our doors and people came. Many came more or less as voluntary immigrants. Others? They came as refugees, forced to flee their homelands because their lives and the lives of their families were endangered. It was not too long before Canada developed a worldwide reputation as a safe haven, epitomized by an act of the United Nations which, as recently as 1986, presented the Nansen Award to the people of Canada for their contribution to "the cause of refugees."

But ironically, in the period since that award was presented, Canadian growth has slowed down. We have been, and still are, in an economic recession. Thousands of people have lost their jobs. Thousands of young graduates from our schools have no hope of finding jobs. This includes the sons and daughters of refugees. Yet Canada still has basically an open-door policy and would wish to rest on its past laurels as a safe haven.

But can Canada still afford to accept new immigrants? Should Canada still remain the safe haven it once was? The exhibit, Safe Haven, does not argue the case one way or the other, but I would stress that there are serious and often persuasive arguments made by both those who favour open and those who favour a more restrictive immigration policy.

The point is that the implications of whatever policy is followed have to be confronted by each of us and by our elected leaders, whether at the federal, provincial, or municipal level. The provocative CBC television documentary just two weeks ago about a Somali community in Toronto's suburb of Etobicoke showed how necessary it is to face this issue head on—and now! I am sure no one here would want parts of Toronto, or any other Canadian city, to be transformed into a South Bronx.

And so, when you leave here tonight, I do not think you should be satisfied. You might have some sense of satisfaction about what Canada has done in the past for refugees, but you must remain troubled about what policy our country should adopt in the future. Look at the pictures, listen to the voices, reflect on the texts. Then follow your consciences and let our leaders know what kind of Canada you would wish to leave your children.

Paul Robert Magocsi
Director and Chief Executive Officer
Multicultural History Society of Ontario
12 November 1993

Afterword

S afe Haven is a collection of the oral testimony of five families who came to Canada as refugees. It is about ordinary people in extraordinary circumstances; it is about survival in the face of overwhelming odds; it is about memory and experience.

Safe Haven is intended as an introduction for the general public to the subject of refugees in Canada through the first-hand accounts of those who have been formally admitted into the country as refugees. Families were selected *not* as representatives of their respective countries but because their stories embodied many aspects of the refugee experience.

The lives of the families in *Safe Haven* were brutally interrupted by military invasion, dictatorship, warfare, and civil conflict. The extremity of such circumstances, the loss of freedom, and the threat to life itself compelled these people to abandon their homes and embark into the unknown in order to survive.

While the general public may be all too aware of the violent events that precipitate refugee movements, frequently nothing more is heard until "alarming" statistics of refugees in Canada are cited by the media. *Safe Haven* is an attempt to bridge this information gap by tracing the difficult decisions, arduous journeys, and diverse adaptations of five refugee families in Canada today.

Those who arrive as refugees must cope with countless adjustments, large and small, required every day in a new country. Abrupt physical displacement also robs new arrivals of their old identities. Even within the same family, each individual–young or old, male or female–has a distinct set of experiences and memories, and responds to change in a manner different from that of other family members. Thus refugees, while dealing with the pressing contingencies of resettlement, are also forced at the same time to redefine themselves at the most fundamental personal level, within the shifting contexts of family, co-ethnic community, and Canadian society. It should come as no surprise that many individuals thus displaced experience, over time, contradictory and vacillating feelings about their homeland, the violence that compelled them to leave, and their new lives in Canada. Indeed, it may be said that these conflicting demands and pressures–many of which are expressed in *Safe Haven*–are hallmarks of the refugee experience.

The families in *Safe Haven* entered Canada as refugees between 1969 and 1991. Although Canada admitted many refugee families such as these during this period, there are few popular publications available about their experiences and the new cultures they bring with them.

In focusing on families from the former Czechoslovakia, Chile, Vietnam, Sri Lanka, and Somalia, it is also possible to trace the changes in refugee-producing situations throughout the world and to follow the development of Canada's refugee programs and policies at home and abroad.

In 1986, the United Nations awarded the Nansen Medal for "the sustained contribution made by the People of Canada to the cause of refugees" and further for the "remarkable achievement of individuals, families, voluntary agencies, community and religious organizations, as well as federal, provincial and municipal authorities in helping refugees to integrate successfully into Canadian society and regain human dignity."

It was the first time the medal was awarded to a people, not to an individual or organization. It is significant that the "showpieces" of Canadian refugee policy over the last decades have almost always been the result of public pressure and lobbying for a more humane and generous response to refugee crises. *Safe Haven* provides a look at one form of refugee assistance: that of refugee resettlement.

Canada has not always welcomed refugees to its shores. But

over the last twenty-five years, Canada has developed more humanitarian refugee policies and programs and has emerged as a leading nation in the admission and resettlement of refugees.

Safe Haven is an acknowledgment of this new Canadian legacy of humanitarianism.

Elizabeth McLuhan
Head of Exhibitions
Multicultural History Society of Ontario

Photo Credits

Cover Photographs

Ethnocultural Voices Series

A Black Man's Toronto, 1914-1980: the Reminiscences of Harry Gairey, edited by Donna Hill

Between Two Worlds: the Autobiography of Stanley Frolick, edited by Lubomyr Luciuk and Marco Carynnyk

The Gordon C. Eby Diaries, 1911-1913: Chronicles of a Mennonite Farmer, edited by James M. Nyce

Heroes of Their Day: the Reminiscences of Bohdan Panchuk, edited by Lubomyr Luciuk

The Finnish Baker's Daughters, by Ali Grönlund Schneider

The Memoirs of Giovanni Veltri, edited by John Potestio

An Ordinary Woman in Extraordinary Times, by Ibolya (Szalai) Grossman

Unhappy Rebel: the Life and Times of Andy Stritof, by Cvetka Kocjancic

Marynia, Don't Cry: Memoirs of Two Polish-Canadian Families, by Apolonja Maria Kojder and Barbara Głogowska

Safe Haven: the Refugee Experience of Five Families, edited by Elizabeth McLuhan